To

From

Date

Just Roll with It

with It

Devotions from the Farmhouse Kitchen

Just Roll with It: Devotions from the Farmhouse Kitchen
© 2019 DaySpring Cards, Inc. All rights reserved.
First Edition, August 2019

Published by:

DaySpring

P.O. Box 1010
Siloam Springs, AR 72761
dayspring.com

Written by: Janice Thompson
Cover and Internal Design: Jessica Wei
Printed in China
Prime: 89897
ISBN: 978-1-68408-625-2

Table of Contents

A Message to Readers

FROM THE FARMHOUSE KITCHEN

Welcome to my wacky, sugarcoated world, y'all! I'm Janice Thompson, Christian author and baker. In my world, books and baking go hand in hand. In my (somewhat messy) kitchen, you're just as likely to find powdered sugar on the countertops as you are to find me wrapping up my latest novel or nonfiction book. That's because I love to bake. Cakes, cookies, candies...you name it, I'm happy to make it.

I'm tickled to invite you into my disheveled domain, where you can watch me stir up sweet treats...and a bit of trouble. Pull up a chair and visit with me while I whip up a multitiered, themed birthday cake or an order of hand-painted cookies. We'll laugh and chat and talk about all the things we're learning about life—and faith—from my baking journey.

Why baking, you ask? Is there any finer way to forget your troubles? One minute you're up to your elbows in flour and sugar; the next you're sprinkling coconut and pecans on a delectable Italian cream cake or sneaking a nibble of that warm-from-the-oven snickerdoodle. One minute you're softening butter in preparation for use; the next you're adding dollops of homemade cream-cheese icing to a luscious red velvet cake.

During those precious in-between moments—with your focus on mixing, scraping, and scooping—life's cares disappear. You're free to give yourself over to the process. There, with only the whirring of the mixer to distract you, God is free to speak into your situation.

And speak He does! He's the Master Chef, after all, and you are His ready student, armed with mixing bowl and whisk. As you're sifting powdered sugar, He's sifting out the pain and turmoil of your day, leaving only peace. As you're rolling out that pie crust or sugar cookie dough, He's teaching you to let the cares of this life roll off you. As you're biting into that oozy chocolate chip cookie, He's reminding you to taste and see that He is still good, no matter what you're facing.

He is good, you know, and longs to meet you wherever you are. But why settle for an ordinary place when you can hang out with Him in the comfort and coziness of your home kitchen? There, between the mixing bowl, the pantry door, and the 350-degree oven, you will find your rhythm. Life will begin to make sense again. Hope will rise inside your soul like bread dough rising in preparation for its eventual journey to the oven.

So grab that rolling pin. Fire up that oven! Tie on your apron! Grab the baking powder, flour, sugar, and other necessities. It's time to head to the kitchen to see what tasty tidbits God has in store for you, His precious child.

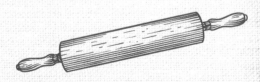

Where There's a Whisk, There's a Way

INTRODUCTION

For the average baker, the kitchen is a place of refuge. It's the place to run when you're fed up with the chaos or you're ready for some concentrated alone time. There, in that comfortable place, you relax. You settle in. Creating yummy treats becomes your mission, and what a mission it is! Cookies. Cakes. Breads. Pies. The task in front of you is all that matters in that moment. You're consumed in a blissful way, swept away in a powdered-sugar haze, with only your baking project in mind.

As you work the bread dough into submission, your mind shifts to a struggle you're having with a friend. God begins to download ideas to rebuild the relationship. As you adjust the temperature on your oven, the Lord reminds you of a recent incident where you got overheated and lost your temper. He whispers, "I can fix that, if you'll let Me." As you pipe buttercream from a bag with a flowery tip, you're reminded of how beautiful life can be when you leave things in God's hands. Yes, there are many opportunities to encounter the Lord in your home kitchen.

No matter how old you are, there are still life lessons to be learned. This learning curve will go on until you've baked that last cake or eaten that last cookie. Submitting yourself to the process of hearing from God is key. He is speaking, even now. There's so much He wants to share—about how much He loves you, how proud He is of you, and what you can do to bring Him great joy. Best of all, you can learn all these things in your cozy kitchen—with flour on your apron and blobs of icing on your cheek.

Wag the Dog

I work with powdered sugar. Lots and lots of powdered sugar. And I'm notorious for getting it all over the place. It's nothing to find the white, fluffy substance on my floor beneath the mixer. You will most certainly locate it on the countertop...even underneath bowls and spoons. I've often found the sticky white powder in my hair after a baking spree! Nothing, however, tops my ultimate powdered sugar story.

I was making frosting for an Italian cream cake and had creamed the butter until it was light and fluffy. I got ready to add the powdered sugar. Apparently, my male dachshund, Copper, decided that this would be the appropriate time to hang out at my feet. (No doubt he was hoping for some overflow!) With the mixer whirring, I added the powdered sugar. *Poof!* The blades were moving so fast that white puffs of sugar shot straight into the air and flew to the ground below, coating everything in sight.

I slowed the mixer and kept working, my thoughts on the frosting, not the dog. Only when I finished mixing the buttercream did I glance down and discover that Copper's back was completely covered in the powdery mist! My black-and-tan Doxie looked like he'd been caught up in a snowstorm. He was absolutely giddy at his good fortune.

Now, dogs have a unique problem that humans don't. They can't reach their own backs. Had he really received this sugary blessing only to find it out of reach? What a sad pooch! There was really no way to clean off the sugar, short of rolling around on the rug.

No problem! My female dachshund, Sasha, showed

up moments later and went to work, cleaning Copper's back. She had a blast, licking off that sweetness. Poor Copper! He got the powdered sugar shower; she got the benefits.

I got to thinking about how many times that has happened in my life. I've come so close to receiving a blessing only to lose it in the eleventh hour to someone else. How sad, to watch as others reap the benefits while I go without.

We have two choices when we face near-miss blessings. We can either grow bitter, or we can hang around at the Master's feet to experience the next overflow. It is coming, you know. He's got blessings in abundance for all of His kids. We've just got to be like Copper, ready to lap it up when the moment comes.

God can pour on the blessings in astonishing ways so that you're ready for anything and everything, more than just ready to do what needs to be done.
II CORINTHIANS 9:8 THE MESSAGE

Prayer

Father, I long to sit at Your feet—not for the blessings You're longing to pour down on me, but simply because I'm Your child. You are my loving Father. You shower me with sweetness when I least expect it. Praise You, Lord, for Your kindness! Amen.

The Boss of That Dough

There's something to be said for coming up with the perfect recipe. I know, because it took me months to do so. When I first started hand-painting sugar cookies, I knew I had to have the perfect cookie recipe. It had to be firm enough to withstand the painting process, particularly the "flooding" of royal icing. But it also had to be soft enough to be enjoyable (and to accentuate the slight crunch of the icing once it dried). The recipe had to be sweet, as all sugar cookies are, but not overly sweet, since the icing would add another sugary layer. Most important, the cookie had to have squared-off edges after baking, leaving me with a flat surface for painting. Most sugar cookie recipes I'd tried had edges that fell off a bit. That would never do.

So, I worked. And worked. And worked some more. I tried a little more of this, a little less of that. Nothing seemed to be just right.

But I finally found my perfect recipe, one that used a combination of sugars (powdered and granulated). My concoction called for a drier dough (using only one egg limits the moisture). My recipe wouldn't take long to chill and would hold its shape during the cutting and baking process. I became the boss of that dough and have mastered it ever since.

It took weeks to get my recipe right, but it was so worth it in the end. Folks seem to love my cookies because they're sweet but not too sweet, soft but still firm enough to hold their shape. I'm happy, too, because the flat surface gives me the perfect palette for painting. It was worth the effort to watch my recipe transform into exactly what I needed it to be.

Isn't that what it's like in our lives, as well? We start out with so many imperfections. Our edges fall off. We're too firm. Or too soft. Or not sweet enough. But God, the Master Baker, keeps working on the recipe until we are transformed into His image. All along the way, we feel the bumps and bruises of the morphing process, but the end result is wonderful! As we become all He created us to be, we leave a sweet taste in the mouths of those whose lives we touch. How sweet, to be transformed into His likeness!

> *Do not conform to the pattern of this world,*
> *but be transformed by the renewing of your mind.*
> *Then you will be able to test*
> *and approve what God's will is—*
> *his good, pleasing and perfect will.*
> ROMANS 12:2 NIV

Prayer

Lord, I know You've had to work hard to shape me into the best possible me I can be. Thank You for not giving up on me, even when my stubbornness and frustrations have prevailed. May I always be a sweet reflection of You, Father. Amen.

A Clogged Tip

If you've ever worked with piping bags, you know what a blessing they can be. Out of such a simple little bag come ribbons of frosting in every color of the rainbow. Scalloped edges, ruffled textures, detailed scrolling...there's a piping tip for every option. And it doesn't matter what sort of frosting you're using—buttercream, royal, Italian meringue—you can create beautiful effects using bags and tips.

I have a love/hate relationship with piping bags. I use them nearly every day of my life, both to trim out cakes and to paint cookies. When working with a wider tip (for cakes, mostly), I do well. But cookies provide interesting challenges.

My icing of choice for cookies is royal, a meringue-based liquid that I flood onto the sugar cookie in the colors of my choice. Only one problem: royal icing is made of powdered sugar, and powdered sugar—even after sifting—forms teensy-tiny clumps inside the piping tip between uses. When I'm using a #2 tip (a pinpoint-sized hole), even a microscopic piece of sugar can get in the way and clog up the works. I know, because it happens to me nearly every time I work with this persnickety icing.

On a particularly difficult day (one of those days when I needed to move swiftly to put out over 250 painted cookies), I found myself with a never-ending clogged tip. I removed the little silver piping tip repeatedly and jabbed a toothpick inside it but just couldn't seem to keep the flow of icing consistent and smooth. Just about the time I started to relax, another clog occured.

As I worked to clear the tip for the hundredth time, I got to thinking about how sometimes life is just like that. There really are times when the good things in our lives (as sweet as sugar, even) get in the way of the "better" things in our lives. Sometimes we make such a big deal out of the blessings, focus on them so intently, that they clog the flow of *other* good things the Lord wants to do in our lives. What a revelation!

What is clogging your tip today? What good thing is getting in the way of what God longs to do in your life? Just something to think about this sweet day.

God is able to bless you abundantly,
so that in all things at all times, having all that you need,
you will abound in every good work.
II CORINTHIANS 9:8 NIV

Prayer

Father, I want the channels of my life to remain wide open so that I can receive all You have for me. Thank You for the reminder that even the blessings in my life can clog up the works if I make them too important. May I always remain open and ready to receive, my eyes focused solely on You and not on the blessings.

Consistency

Royal icing is a pain to work with. There's no other way to say it. Add half a teaspoon too much water to the batch and the icing flows right off the edge of the cookie. Get it too thick and it won't spread out at all. Instead, it clumps up in ugly little mounds. On the rough days, it feels like I spend half my baking time working and reworking icing to make sure it's consistent, one color to the next. This is particularly troublesome when working with multiple layers and colors. Every single color has to be perfect. And trust me, I'm far from perfect.

Early one morning I dove into what I thought would be a simple project—two dozen birthday cookies for a two-year-old. Such a fun project: twelve hearts and twelve cupcake-shaped sugar cookies, hand-painted in pink, purple, and white. I could've done them in my sleep.

Or so I thought.

I stirred the icings until they reached what felt and looked like flood consistency (basically the same consistency as honey). Then I poured the icings into bags, according to color. I used #2 tips (my norm for flooding) and sat down to begin the process of icing the cookies. Imagine my surprise when the icing began to pour out of the bag like water. Ugh.

I reached for a smaller tip (a #1), knowing that would slow the dribbling. Unfortunately, it didn't help. The wet icing still ran down the sides of the cookies, creating a mess on the tray below. In frustration, I emptied the icing from the bag and added powdered sugar to thicken things up a bit. It still didn't come out right.

In the end, the cookies looked great. But they took me double the time to ice because I had to keep going back with a paper towel, cleaning up my mess.

Can't you envision God, our Master Baker, standing nearby with paper towels in hand? Surely He looks at our inconsistencies (passionate in our faith one day, waning the next; up with our emotions one day, down the next) and patiently takes the time to clean up our messes. Today, as you strive to follow hard after the Lord, ask Him to show you how to be consistent in your walk. Trust me, there will be fewer messes to clean up in the end!

> *Therefore, my beloved brothers,*
> *be steadfast, immovable, always abounding*
> *in the work of the Lord, knowing that*
> *in the Lord your labor is not in vain.*
> I CORINTHIANS 15:58 ESV

Lord, I want to be consistent. I don't want to cause You more work. Thank You for Your patience, Father, as You continue to work in my life. Amen.

Kitchen Celebration

I didn't mean to scare the yardman. Really, I didn't. It was just one of those days when I felt like praising the Lord while baking. With a full day's work ahead of me, I needed energizing, and I needed it now. I turned on some of my favorite worship music. Loud. Okay, *really* loud. Then I got busy in the kitchen, making cookies for customers.

Ordinarily, a cookie order of that magnitude would overwhelm me, but not on this particular day. The lyrics to the songs drew me in, and before long I found myself singing and dancing around the kitchen, arms outstretched—mixing spoon in one hand, parchment paper in the other.

On and on I went, singing at the top of my lungs, my worship a song of abandon to the Lord. In between choruses I rolled out cookies, put them on trays, and loaded them into the oven. Before long, I'd made a mess. A big mess.

What I sight I must've been, covered in smudges of flour, powdered sugar, and butter! Not that I minded. Oh, no. I did the work in front of me, then went right back to singing.

Little did I know, the yardman was hard at work in my backyard, just beyond the window...the one with the wide-open blinds. When I clapped eyes on him, I panicked.

Oops!

Okay, maybe he saw me, maybe he didn't. But for a moment there, I almost stopped worshiping completely. I got embarrassed. Did he perhaps wonder if, I'd lost my mind, singing at the top of my lungs like that? Did he think I was in some sort of physical distress? If so, he didn't show it. He just kept working on the yard, seemingly oblivious to my ponderings.

Has that ever happened to you? Have you ever praised God publicly, only to feel silly after the fact? God wants us to be bold in our faith and joyous in our worship. Who cares if the yardman sees? Maybe he'll be so inspired that he will take up singing while he mows. (One never knows!) Regardless, keep on praising. Keep on singing. Let nothing hinder your praise!

Praise Him with tambourines and dancing;
praise Him with stringed instruments and flutes.
Praise Him with loud cymbals;
praise Him with crashing cymbals.
Let everything that breathes praise the LORD.
PSALM 150:4–6 NCV

Prayer

Father, I love to praise You! It doesn't matter if I'm in my kitchen, in my closet, or standing next to fellow parishioners in church. Singing songs of worship, lifting Your name in praise...these are my favorite things to do. One day, Lord, I'll get to worship for all eternity. Until then, I hope You don't mind if I sing and dance while baking, my rolling pin in one hand and my spatula in the other! What joy, to praise Your holy name! Amen.

The Naked Cake

It's a fascinating trend: naked cakes. You've seen them, no doubt. They're usually four tiers high—layers and layers of white cake with virtually no frosting, only what we bakers like to call the "clear coat"—a thin/transparent layer that seals in crumbs.

What is the point of the naked cake, you ask? Well, it's perfect for the bride and groom who aren't fond of frosting. (Do such people really exist? How can a person eat cake without frosting, I ask you?) Others choose naked cakes for their rustic/natural aesthetic. They cover the tiers with fresh berries and greenery and sprinkle a bit of powdered sugar on top. Voilà! You feel like you've wandered into the forest where the wood nymphs are ready to serve you a slice of their handmade cake creation.

I was recently asked to bake my first-ever naked cake for a baby shower. I got excited about the fact that I wouldn't have to whip up gallons of homemade buttercream (always a task in itself).

Now, there's only one problem with unfrosted cakes: You can see every flaw. If the layers don't line up properly, if the edges of one cake are a slightly different color than the others...it all shows. And heaven knows, we bakers don't like our flaws to show. We do everything in our power to cover up the boo-boos.

I gave it my best shot, cooking each cake exactly the same length of time to assure perfect coloring from top tier to bottom. In the end, my first naked cake wasn't perfect, but it was pretty close. The mother-to-be loved the cake...and so did I! (Go figure.)

Maybe you can relate. You are human, after all! And like all humans, you're flawed. It's one thing to cover our flaws and another to have them flaunted for all to see. When others see us for who we are, they see our burnt edges, our uneven layers, our wonky flaws. We feel vulnerable, exposed. We'd rather hide away those things, thank you very much.

Oh, but isn't that what makes the body of Christ so wonderful? Wouldn't it be boring if everyone was perfect? Today, why not let down your hair a little? Dare to be vulnerable around the people you love. Let them see the real you, wrinkles and all. Chances are, they'll love you all the more.

Not that I have already obtained all this,
or have already arrived at my goal,
but I press on to take hold of that for
which Christ Jesus took hold of me.
PHILIPPIANS 3:12 NIV

Prayer

Lord, I feel so flawed sometimes. I do my best not to show off my rough edges, but sometimes they're hard to hide. Thank You for giving me permission to just be myself around You, Father. You cover my imperfections with Your grace (a lovely "clear coat") and assure me that I'm loved, flaws and all! Praise You, Lord. Amen.

Cracked Eggs

My intentions were good—crack the eggs directly over the mixing bowl and let them fall in, one at a time, as the blades whir in the background. Ordinarily I'm a skilled egg-cracker. (I hate to brag, but I excel at one-handed egg-cracking. My grandchildren are mesmerized.) But back to my story. The first egg went in just fine. The second, also fine. That third egg, though? It had a little crack in it. I didn't really spend much time fretting over it. What harm could a little crack do, after all?

I split the shell and let the egg tumble directly into the batter, only to discover a fiasco. What seemed perfectly fine on the outside was a bacteria-filled mess on the inside. The innards were brown and stinky, not at all what I was expecting. Ew! Horror washed over me as I realized the inevitable: that egg was spoiled and had tainted my batter, which meant I had to start completely over.

Maybe you can relate to this story. Your walk with God is going along just fine. All is well. Then, over time, little cracks begin to enter into your relationship with Him. You don't even notice them at first, that's how small they are. Over time, they become more obvious, but by then you've developed poor habits. It's easier to compromise than to do the right thing. You don't have time to pray. You back away from Christian friends. You miss a few church services. You let your Bible get dusty. None of these things are overt sins. They're just teensy-tiny cracks. But before long, things get stinky.

A little breach in a shell can have devastating effects, but here's the good news: it's never too late with God! He can take a bacteria-filled egg (spiritually speaking) and make it new again. He longs to seal up those cracks and make all things new in your relationship with Him so that you never grow stagnant, stale, or broken.

What cracks needs to be sealed today? Give them to God and watch Him make you healthy and strong once again.

So whoever knows the right thing to do
and fails to do it, for him it is sin.
JAMES 4:17 ESV

Prayer

Lord, I'm sorry for the compromises I've made. I don't want any area of my walk with You to be spoiled. I want to be solid in my commitment, not slipping up. Thank You for the reminder to stay strong in You. Amen.

Low on Sugar

My weekly shopping excursions are pretty humorous. I load up my basket with the necessary ingredients: flour, sugar, powdered sugar, oil, butter, baking powder, eggs, and so on. When I reach the cash register, I get lots of stares and (always) the same question: "What are you baking?" I usually respond with the words, "What was your first clue that I'm baking something?" Then we both laugh.

The truth is, I go through a lot of ingredients. It's impossible to imagine that the sixty eggs I purchased last week are already gone at the beginning of this week, but it's true. And the ten pounds of butter I bought the last time I went to the grocery store? It disappeared, too.

Perhaps the one ingredient I purchase more than any other is powdered sugar. I use it in sugar cookies and royal icing (for the cookies) and for buttercream. I also use it in homemade fondant. It's not unusual for me to go through ten to fifteen bags of powdered sugar per week. So, when I recently found myself with less than a cup of powdered sugar in the house, I couldn't believe it. Running out of the powdery white substance is something akin to running out of water. It's simply impossible to function without it.

On the night in question, I was nearly done with my final baking job of the day and just needed enough powdered sugar to roll out my decorative fondant pieces. I used a tablespoon at a time, being oh so careful to conserve. Thankfully, I finished the project with about a quarter cup of powdered sugar left over. Whew!

Imagine my surprise a few days later when I discovered a grocery store bag full of ingredients in the back of my pantry. Inside—you guessed it—was one bag of powdered sugar. It was there all along.

That's how life is, isn't it? We feel depleted, as if we can't go on. Our energy is waning. Our "want to" is gone. Our battery has drained.

Then we remember...God is our source. He's our strength. We'll never run dry. We'll never go without! He's got all we need and more. All we have to do is ask.

What are you lacking today? Reach into your spiritual pantry and pull out what you need. You'll never go without when the Master Baker is at work in your life.

> *My God will meet all your needs according*
> *to the riches of His glory in Christ Jesus.*
> PHILIPPIANS 4:19 NIV

Prayer

Father, I know what it feels like to be depleted, to think I don't have the wherewithal to go on. I've been at that point frequently, Lord. Thank You for the reminder that I'll never go without as long as I remain plugged in to You. What an amazing provider You are, Lord! Amen.

Give It Up

I'd taken on two jobs in one day—cookies and a cake, both beach/water themed. The cookies were a tougher design than most, very meticulous and time-consuming. I put off working on the cake until after I'd completed three dozen of the beach-themed sugar cookies. In fact, I don't think I even got rolling on the cake until around eleven that night.

The inside of the cake was multicolored, which is a bit more time-consuming. And the cake had to be frosted in buttercream to resemble a beach scene, complete with water, waves, shoreline, and sand. Then, of course, I had to add the beach decor—umbrellas, floaties, etc. Whew.

I felt my energy begin to wane somewhere around 1:45 in the morning. In fact, I was so exhausted I couldn't even think straight. I proclaimed the project complete at 2:00 a.m. Only one problem: my kitchen was a wreck. I needed to get the mess cleaned up before I could go to bed.

Only, I was half asleep already. In my current state, I could barely remember my own name, let alone where things were supposed to go. I left the dishwasher door open and loaded the dirty bowls, decorating tools, and baking pans. From across the kitchen island I caught sight of an oversized knife, which I'd used to cut the cake board. *I'd better get it into the dishwasher, too,* I thought.

I never made it.

Oh, I managed to get the knife into my hand, but as I headed back toward the dishwasher, I tripped...and down I went, fifteen-inch knife with me. Thankfully, the knife shot across the room and landed underneath my baker's shelf. I'd been spared. But what a close call!

Have you ever put yourself into a precarious position due to exhaustion? When we pass the point of no return, when we refuse to give it up, we're of no use to ourselves or to others. And burnout can lead to accidents. Thank goodness, I didn't have any lasting injuries (though I was achy and bruised the following morning). But things might have ended badly, and all because I didn't know how to quit. Perhaps there's a life lesson there. Next time I'll think twice before baking in my sleep!

Come to Me, all you who are weary and burdened,
and I will give you rest. Take My yoke upon you and learn
from Me, for I am gentle and humble in heart,
and you will find rest for your souls.
For My yoke is easy and My burden is light.
MATTHEW 11:28–30 NIV

Prayer

Lord, thank You for the reminder that my body wasn't meant to run 24/7. I want to be of use to You, Father, but I won't be if I'm burning the candle at both ends. Remind me, in the moment, that rest is more important than any project I might need to tackle.

The Secret Ingredient

Every baker has a secret or two up her sleeve. Each one adds her own "special something" to the cake batter, cookie dough, or pie crust, something of a personal choosing. When others marvel at the taste, the chef quietly nods and whispers, "Secret ingredient." And she never, under any circumstance, gives it away.

How mysterious. How fun! And how creative, to always keep folks guessing!

For years I've added a "secret ingredient" to my buttercream. Only recently have I revealed it to the masses. I didn't really mind sharing, because I wanted folks to have the same opportunity on their end to have a tasty outcome. Most of my customers know that my buttercream frosting almost always has a small amount of cream cheese in it, but that's not the secret ingredient. Nope. Not even close. Want to guess?

If you said, "Italian Sweet Crème coffee creamer," you would be correct! Only, I'm guessing you *didn't* say that at all, did you? It's a random addition, one most nonbakers would never think of. The truth is, buttercreams can get too stiff if you overdo the powdered sugar. Some bakers add a bit of milk or cream to thin it down. Those who don't have the option of refrigerating their cakes might add water. But me? I use Italian Sweet Crème creamer. It has just the right flavors to complement my already-a-bit-different-from-the-norm buttercream. And folks seem to love it.

I got to thinking about this and realized that God has a "secret ingredient" too (though He reveals it in His Word, for those who are paying attention). It's one that sweetens any friendship, mends fractured relationships, does away with bitterness, and calms raging (emotional) seas.

That secret ingredient? Forgiveness.

You could live your life without it, of course, but the outcome wouldn't be as tasty. If you add forgiveness (even when it's hard) then God will forgive you in exchange. That's an amazing offering, isn't it?

Who do you need to forgive today? Take the time to talk to Jesus about it, then forgive and let go. And while you're at it, why not bake that person a dozen cupcakes? Just be sure to add Italian Sweet Crème creamer to the frosting!

When you stand praying,
if you hold anything against anyone, forgive them,
so that your Father in heaven may forgive you your sins.
MARK 11:25 NIV

Prayer

Lord, forgiveness is one ingredient I often (deliberately) leave out. It's not always easy to forgive. I'm grateful for the reminder, though, because I realize that You can't forgive me until I forgive others. Today I choose to do just that. Help me, Lord. I can't do it on my own. Amen.

Substitutions

I do it all the time—substitute one ingredient for another. When I'm short on butter, I throw in a little shortening. When I don't have real vanilla, I use artificial. Out of cream of tartar? I combine baking soda and baking powder. Trying to limit sugars? Throw in some applesauce. Giving up on carbs so that I can drop a few pounds or keep my blood sugar in check? Use almond flour or coconut flour. I've become quite a whiz at swapping one item for another.

The truth is, substitutions are okay, but they're not the preferred ingredient. Nothing tops real butter or vanilla. And though applesauce is sweet, it doesn't have the same flavor as that bad-for-you granulated sugar. Substitute flours are an acquired taste and many people don't notice the difference, but I always do.

Oftentimes my substitutions lead to not-so-great cookies or cakes. Oh, they're tolerable. And they dress up just as nicely when you cover them with buttercream or fondant. But they don't taste the same and the texture is off. (There's nothing more disappointing to a baker than a product that is almost-but-not-quite what they'd hoped.) Give me the real deal any day.

In like manner, sometimes we make substitutions in our spiritual life, too. Instead of running to God with our problems, we run to a friend or social media. There's nothing wrong with that, unless we're looking for all our answers there. There are other ways we substitute, as well. When we're stressed, we reach for junk food. When we're depressed, we hide away and binge-watch our favorite shows instead of getting real with the Lord. These are all poor substitutions for what we really need, which is time with Him to sort things out.

Today, acknowledge your need for the real deal. No substitutions. What's the first thing on your list?

> *But seek first the kingdom of God*
> *and his righteousness,*
> *and all these things*
> *will be added to you.*
> MATTHEW 6:33 ESV

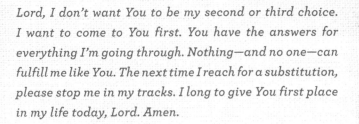

Prayer

Lord, I don't want You to be my second or third choice. I want to come to You first. You have the answers for everything I'm going through. Nothing—and no one—can fulfill me like You. The next time I reach for a substitution, please stop me in my tracks. I long to give You first place in my life today, Lord. Amen.

An Explosion of Jealousy

Contrary to popular belief, I don't always bake everything from scratch. While preparing breakfast for my family one morning, I placed an unopened can of store-bought biscuits on the counter, then left the room to tend to something else. Suddenly I heard a terrible explosion. It sounded like a gunshot. I raced to the kitchen, kids right behind me. Imagine our surprise! Biscuits covered the entire room. There were biscuits on the wall, biscuits on the counter, and biscuits on the floor. None of us dared move until we were sure the explosion had fully ended.

Jealousy, if left untended, is a little like that. We do our best to tuck envy into the secret places, thinking we've got it all under control. Then something happens and the pressure begins to build—a coworker gets a raise, someone else gets the promotion we were expecting, a friend gets a new car or house. Instead of humbling ourselves and offering congratulations, the biscuits come shooting out of the can. We make a tremendous amount of noise and mess up everything in sight. We leave a shocked audience to clean up after us.

How do we stop jealousy? It must be diffused at its root. If we live as servants, as Christ instructed, there is no room left for jealousy. Out of a pure heart, we celebrate the victories of others. We wash their feet *especially* when it's hard. And we do it not out of obligation, but from a pure heart...a servant's heart.

Sure, there will be plenty of opportunities to forget

that it's not all about us. But we have to make a conscious effort not to let the pressure build to the danger point. Otherwise, those biscuits will mess up a perfectly lovely room.

> *Therefore, rid yourselves*
> *of all malice and all deceit, hypocrisy,*
> *envy, and slander of every kind.*
> I PETER 2:1 NIV

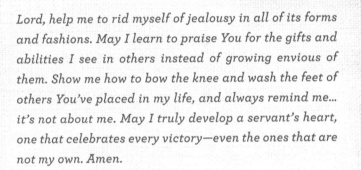

Prayer

Lord, help me to rid myself of jealousy in all of its forms and fashions. May I learn to praise You for the gifts and abilities I see in others instead of growing envious of them. Show me how to bow the knee and wash the feet of others You've placed in my life, and always remind me... it's not about me. May I truly develop a servant's heart, one that celebrates every victory—even the ones that are not my own. Amen.

Procrastibaking

Iknow, I know...there's no such word as *procrastibaking*. Well, there is now. I've always been good at procrastinating, putting things off until the eleventh hour, but never more so than since I started baking. House needs to be cleaned? Perfect time to bake some cupcakes! Laundry needs to be folded? I'd prefer to stir up a batch of snickerdoodles, thank you very much. Bills need to be paid? I'd rather order baking supplies online. (I've been wanting some new cookie cutters anyway.) In need of a good night's sleep? I'd rather watch cake- and cookie-decorating videos on YouTube. Vacuum needs to be run? Feels like the perfect time to bake some cupcakes for the grandkids. I can think of a thousand ways to while away the hours, avoiding what needs to be done.

The truth is, baking is more fun than working (or sleeping). Now, I know what some of you are thinking: baking is work. For the average Joe, sure. But for those of us with buttercream running through our veins, baking is as natural as breathing. We do it to relax and rarely consider it work. That's why we're willing to lay down other obligations to do what we love. It would be something akin to skipping the dishes to watch your favorite show on TV. Of course, the cleanup after the fact feels like a task worth putting off, but not the baking itself. Most of the bakers I know would rather dream up their next project than fold laundry or mop floors any day.

What about you, friend? Are you a procrastibaker? Have you ever used time that should have been slotted for other tasks to bake cookies, cake, or pie instead?

Have you ever whiled away the hours, wasting time instead of tackling a personal or household project? We all need to maintain discipline, or the important things will never get done. What's one thing you've been putting off? Maybe today is the day to finally dive in and see that task to completion.

For the moment all discipline
seems painful rather than pleasant,
but later it yields the peaceful fruit of righteousness
to those who have been trained by it.
HEBREWS 12:11 ESV

Prayer

Lord, I want to be diligent, not just in my relationship with You but also in the tasks You've given me. I don't want to be a time-waster. Thank You for shining Your light on this issue. May I be diligent to do all You've put in front of me and not procrastinate. Amen.

The Perfect Sugar Cookie

CREAM TOGETHER

- 2 sticks (1 cup) *real butter* (no substitutions)
- 1 extra large egg
- 1 cup powdered sugar
- ½ cup granulated sugar
- 1 teaspoon vanilla
- ½ teaspoon almond extract

IN A SEPARATE BOWL WHISK TOGETHER

- 3 cups flour
- 1 teaspoon baking powder
- ½ teaspoon salt

INSTRUCTIONS

Slowly add flour mixture to butter/sugar/eggs.

Put the dough into a ziplock bag and chill in the freezer for 15 minutes or the in refrigerator for 30–60 minutes.

Put waxed paper on the counter and set a portion of the dough on it. Set another piece of waxed paper on top of the dough. Time to grab your rolling pin! Using doubled paint sticks as guides, roll out the dough and use cookie cutters to cut.

Bake at 375°F for 10 minutes or your preference. Don't overbake.

Cool on racks until room temperature. Don't attempt to decorate until the cookies are completely cooled.

Royal Icing

INGREDIENTS

- 4½ tablespoons meringue powder
- ½ cup + 2 tablespoons water
- 1 teaspoon cream of tartar
- 1 teaspoon vanilla
- ½ teaspoon almond extract
- 1 bag powdered sugar (7–8 cups)

INSTRUCTIONS

Put all items except powdered sugar into mixing bowl. Mix until frothy (less than a minute). Add full bag powdered sugar and mix until incorporated (a few seconds). Turn mixer on low and beat for 10 minutes nonstop until it reaches a meringue-like consistency. Immediately cover with plastic wrap (touching the icing) and a damp towel above that.

Now it's time to color your icing. Scoop out about a cup of the icing into a small bowl and add your coloring gel. (Don't use water-based food colorings, as they add liquid to the recipe.) Mix thoroughly. Add bits of water (one droplet at a time) to get the colored icing to piping (toothpaste) consistency. Scoop out half of it and put it into a piping bag with a #2 tip. With the remaining icing in the bowl, add tiny bits of water (stirring nonstop by hand) until it reaches honey consistency. You know you've reached the right consistency when you can drag a knife through it and it takes about 10 seconds for the line to close up again.

Italian Cream Cake

Here's a quick-and-easy version of my very favorite cake. It's guaranteed to make your family swoon.

INGREDIENTS

- 1 white (or yellow) cake mix
- 3 eggs
- 1 stick butter, softened
- ½ cup shortening
- 1 cup water
- 1 teaspoon vanilla extract
- 1 small box instant vanilla pudding
- 1 cup flaked coconut, plain or toasted
- 1 cup chopped pecans

INSTRUCTIONS

Place dry cake mix into a mixing bowl and add butter and shortening. Incorporate three eggs and one cup of water, then add vanilla. Add the instant vanilla pudding (dry) and cream until smooth. Slowly work in the flaked coconut and chopped pecans.

Separate into two 8-inch round pans and bake at 350°F until done (approximately 30 minutes).

Frost with my cream cheese buttercream recipe and top with pecans and coconut. Decorate with frosting swirls.

Janice's Cream Cheese Buttercream

CREAM TOGETHER

- 3 sticks butter (softened)
- One 8-ounce block cream cheese

WHEN THOROUGHLY BLENDED, ADD

- 7–8 cups powdered sugar

TO THIN OUT, ADD

- Italian Sweet Crème creamer (to taste)

If you're using this recipe to decorate (e.g., rosettes or other designs that require stabilization), add 1 cup/rectangle of high-quality shortening to the recipe and hold back on the creamer. You'll need the stability of the shortening to make the buttercream designs hold their shape.

Variations on American Buttercream

America is known for its sweet, creamy buttercream—a simple mixture of whipped butter and powdered sugar. If you really want to jazz up your buttercream, here are some simple ways to do so:

- To make chocolate buttercream, add chocolate ganache or ⅓ cup cocoa powder.

- To make raspberry buttercream, add pureed raspberry preserves (and adjust powdered sugar as necessary).

- To make lemon buttercream, add lemon curd.

- For cookies-and-cream buttercream, add smashed Oreos (or other cookies of choice).

- For butter-pecan buttercream, add maple syrup and pecans.

Tips for Great Cookie Decorating

- Create a clean, well-prepped decorating station. I always have my piping bags, bottles, toothpicks, napkins, extra tips, etc., before I begin. I also use a cutting mat (or waxed paper) on the countertop.

- Outline your cookies with piping-consistency icing, then set aside (on cookie sheets or cooling racks) to dry before flooding. (I use an oscillating fan on my cookies as they dry. It speeds up the process.)

- After flooding your cookies, tap them gently to work out any air bubbles. You can also use toothpicks to pop any air bubbles. Do this right away.

- Speaking of toothpicks, keep several on hand. The piping tips often clog as you work.

- If you're adding multiple colors to your cookies, let each color dry (with the fan blowing on them) and then add the next color.

- Let the cookies dry for five to seven hours before packaging. They could and should be left out in the open (not closed up or covered) during the drying process. Many people worry that the cookies will grow stale but the opposite occurs! The royal icing locks in the freshness of the cookie and it's just as yummy hours later.

Common Baking Substitutions

We don't always have what we need on hand when we're baking, but that's okay. Why not use a substitution instead?

Consider the following:

- If the recipe calls for cream of tartar and you're out of it, use equal parts baking powder and baking soda to create your own.

- Off of sugar but you want to sweeten those muffins or banana bread? Consider unsweetened applesauce as a replacement.

- Trying to cut back on carbs? Choose a different flour (like almond, coconut, or oat bran) instead of the traditional white flour.

- Counting calories? There are many sugar substitutes available that work well for baking (replacing both white sugar and brown).

- If you're out of flour and you need to grease/flour a cake pan, use the dry boxed cake mix instead.

- To make your cake fluffier, use 4 egg whites in place of 3 whole eggs and whip slightly before adding to the mix.

- Out of buttermilk? Make your own by adding 1 teaspoon of either vinegar or lemon juice to a cup of milk. Let stand for 5 minutes.

- Out of cake flour? Sift ¾ cup all-purpose flour with 2 tablespoons cornstarch.

- Cutting back on eggs? Try 3 tablespoons of mayonnaise in place of one egg.

If we are what we eat, then I am awfully sweet.

ANONYMOUS

Keep Calm and Bake

INTRODUCTION

Even for the best of bakers, things don't always go as planned. Cakes fall flat. Egg whites refuse to reach their peak. Bread doughs sit in lumps, determined not to rise. Royal icing refuses to dry because it's raining outside. It's frustrating to have to start over, especially if you're in a time crunch or you plan for others to enjoy your creation at a special event. Talk about stressful! You want to cry, to scream, to climb into bed and pull the covers over your head. This is more than an inconvenience; it's a catastrophe!

But before you toss that batter into the trash can, pause for a moment and think about what you've learned from the experience. Between the cookie crumbs, the lumpy frosting, and the burned-up mixer, there are lessons to be learned. Every lesson will make you a better baker...and perhaps a better person.

How you respond to unforeseen kitchen calamities—whether great or small—is an indicator of how you'll respond to the bigger, more important things in life. Don't be too hard on yourself when things start to crumble! Just go with the flow and try to see each little adventure for what it is—an opportunity to grow in your craft. God wants you to enjoy the process, even when the cookie crumbles, the pie crust shrinks, or the birthday cake is topsy-turvy. Every imperfection is another opportunity to acknowledge that you're only human. (And isn't it gratifying to know that the people eating that lopsided cake are only human, as well?)

Sure, you want to do your best work. But sometimes accidents happen. Things go wrong even when you think all your ducks are perfectly aligned. There's still plenty of joy in the journey if you just keep calm and bake.

The Upside-Down Cake

I was commissioned by my daughter's best friend to make her wedding cake, but nothing about the baking process went as planned. I ended up tossing and remaking the various layers of cake multiple times. Somehow I managed to get the layers constructed and iced, ready to be delivered and assembled at the venue.

On the day of the delivery, the cake came together seamlessly. The four-tiered beauty stood graceful and tall. I gave the lovely cake one last glance before leaving for the off-site ceremony. What a relief!

What a shock, an hour later, to return to the reception venue to find the cake table empty. Yes, empty! Where I'd once seen a lovely, four-tiered wonder, I now saw a blank table. I didn't want to believe it, but my beautiful wedding cake was MIA.

After a bit of frantic scrambling, I learned the awful truth: the cake had tumbled shortly after I left. The waiters, God bless them, had managed to salvage the bottom two tiers, which were hiding in the kitchen, and had already sliced up the top two.

I was devastated. And embarrassed. And ashamed. How could I ever face this bride with the news? With my extra piping bag in hand, I managed to "fix" what was left of the bottom two tiers, but they looked awful. (Truly awful.) In fact, one elderly male guest looked down at my finished product and, with a rich Texas twang, said, "Is *that* the weddin' cake?" Ugh.

Thank goodness, the bride took it all in stride. The guests seemed a bit perplexed...until the cake was served. I was stunned to discover that ice-cold slice of cake to be the best thing I'd ever put in my mouth. The guests agreed. What I'd lacked in structure, I made up for in taste.

In retrospect, I realized that the foundation of the cake was not secure. I hadn't braced the tiers appropriately with the necessary dowels and boards. From that point on, every tiered cake I've baked has been adequately built/supported from the bottom up.

What a life lesson! When our lives are built on Christ, the solid Rock, we stand strong and tall. But when we build our lives on sand—things that shift to and fro—we're like that wedding cake: we tumble to the ground. No matter how beautiful things are on the outside, it's what's on the inside that counts.

Is your cake standing strong today? Have you built your life on the Rock? Today is a great day to root yourself in Him so that you can stand strong no matter what comes your way.

He's solid rock under my feet, breathing room for my soul,
an impregnable castle: I'm set for life.
My help and glory are in God.
PSALM 62:6-7 THE MESSAGE

Prayer

Lord, be my support! I plant my feet on solid ground today, Father, and ask that You hold me steady, no matter what comes my way. Amen.

The Day the Mountain Crumbled

It started out like any other day: Bake a multi-tiered cake as a gift for a local foster kids' ministry. Construct the cake. Load the cake into the back of the SUV. Head to venue. But what started out as ordinary ended up as anything but when I made a (slow, carefully executed) left-hand turn onto the feeder of the Grand Parkway.

I heard the crash and my heart sank. I immediately pictured the beautiful four-tiered Frozen/winter-themed cake smashed to bits in the back of my vehicle. I pulled into the nearest parking lot and opened the rear of my SUV to discover that the top three tiers had separated from the bottom and were lying on their sides. My winter mountain had crumbled, and there was nothing I could do about it. The children at the apartment complex would never see the cake I'd spent hours working on for their Christmas party.

Or would they?

As I stared at the mess in front of me, I realized that the top three tiers were probably reparable. I'd have to turn the car around and head home to tackle the job, but I had plenty of time. Showing up with a smaller cake wouldn't really be that big of a deal anyway. When I arrived home, I decided the bottom cake might also be fixable, so I filled a big hole with buttercream (shh! Don't tell!) and stuck the toy figures on top. Voilà!

When I arrived at the venue a short time later, the kids were delighted with my two cakes. They never knew (or cared) that my original masterpiece had crumbled. Instead, they dove in and ate cake...and lots of it!

Maybe you can relate. Maybe you're loaded with big ideas. You've built "mighty mountains" in your mind. Perhaps you've already witnessed some crumbling. Never fear! God can take our messes and turn them into messages. Just add buttercream and serve with a smile!

> *I have said these things to you,*
> *that in me you may have peace.*
> *In the world you will have tribulation.*
> *But take heart;*
> *I have overcome the world.*
> JOHN 16:33 ESV

Prayer

Lord, I know I can't control when things go wrong. I have big plans and sometimes things topple. But You're such a creative God! You can piece my mountains back together and make them better than ever. I'm so grateful, Father. Amen.

Out to Pasture

My niece loves horses, so I decided to bake a "pasture"-themed cake for her birthday. It wasn't terribly difficult to bake a large rectangular cake and cover it with green buttercream. I then added a couple of "ponds" (surrounded by fondant rocks) and bales of hay (tiny barrel-shaped bits of fondant covered in straw-colored, hay-like strips of buttercream). I trimmed out the edges of the cake with a darker green, using a grass tip, and even put a couple of "hilly" spots on it, as well as some tiny fondant flowers along the edge of the pond.

I'd purchased a set of miniature plastic horses online, just the right size to add to my pasture. They arrived in excellent shape. I put them into place on the cake in strategic positions. A couple of them nibbled on bales of hay. A few drank from the ponds. Some ate grass in the field.

I decided my pasture needed a fence, so I melted dark chocolate and piped "rails," which I pieced together to form a large rectangular fence all around the cake. I was genuinely amazed at the outcome. Wow.

Of course, I had to transport the cake to my niece's home, so I eased it into the back of my SUV and drove with extra care, arriving forty minutes later.

Sadly, I discovered that a portion of my fence had broken in transport. The horses were free to roam! They had no boundaries. I did my best to piece the broken bits together once I got the cake set up, but one section was too far gone. So I set one of the horses outside the opening, as if I'd done it all on purpose.

That pasture cake reminds me so much of my relationship with the Lord. He gives me boundaries. Safety zones. I read them in His Word. He places His law in my mind and heart so that I never forget. He says, "This far, and no farther." Sadly, I often try to stray outside the barriers and sometimes land in trouble (much like that horse outside the fence). Thank goodness we serve an amazing, forgiving God, who sweeps us back into the family (pasture) and begins the process of training all over again.

"This is the covenant
I will make with the people of Israel after that time,"
declares the LORD.
"I will put My law in their minds
and write it on their hearts. I will be their God,
and they will be My people."
JEREMIAH 31:33 NIV

Prayer

I'll admit it, Lord. Sometimes I stray. I know Your Word. I know the boundaries that are meant to protect me. But, like that horse on the outside edge of the fence, I long to see what's on the other side. Thanks for reminding me that one day with You (inside Your pasture) is better than a thousand elsewhere. Amen.

Don't Rain on My Minion

I love baking for friends, and I especially love creating yummy delights for their children's birthdays. When a good friend asked me to bake a Minion cake for her son, I jumped at the chance. This would be a tricky one, completely rounded on top and covered in fondant (not my specialty). Still, I was willing to give it a shot to bring a smile to a little boy's face.

Thankfully, the cake came together just fine. On the day of the party, however, a storm blew in. Ordinarily this wouldn't be a problem, but this party happened to be held at a local pizza parlor and I had to deliver the cake without a box, since I couldn't find one to fit such a tall, odd-shaped cake. Our home had an attached garage, so I didn't have any trouble getting the cake into my car without getting soaked. However, when I arrived at the venue, torrential rains were pouring down and the wind was blowing like mad. Instead of carrying the cake in, I went inside and explained the situation. We opted to have dinner first and wait to see if the storm would pass.

It didn't.

When the time came to fetch the cake, I did my best. My daughter carried an umbrella and we tried to keep that cake dry. Unfortunately, the sideways rain soaked the fondant and our little minion looked more like a woman with cheap mascara after a good cry. We ate it anyway, and it tasted fantastic! Everyone raved at the yummy cake.

Isn't that just how life is? You plan for a big event and then a storm (literal or figurative) blows in, messing up your plans. You can't fix it. There's no way to make it look pretty once again. But if you forge ahead, you'll see that something sweet can still come out it. So let the storms blow. The cake will still be just as sweet.

> *He made the storm be still,*
> *and the waves of the sea were hushed.*
> PSALM 107:29 ESV

Prayer

Father, I'm such a mess sometimes. Storms blow in and wreak havoc. I stumble around, soaked to the bone. I can't even pretend to make my situation look pretty. But You, Lord, still bring sweetness even after the storm. Have I mentioned how grateful I am? Praise You, Lord. Amen.

A Distracted Shopping Trip

One afternoon I went to a large grocery store to buy ingredients. As I walked in, I tossed my purse into an empty basket and headed to the produce department. I chatted on the phone with a friend as I shopped. I'd just tossed some carrots into my basket when I realized my purse had gone missing. Ack! I saw my produce in the basket...but no purse. I immediately went into a panic. I told my friend I'd have to call her back, that someone had stolen my purse.

In a panic, I took off out of the store, heading straight to my car to see if I'd left my purse inside. About halfway out to the car I realized I was pushing the basket with the groceries in it...groceries I hadn't paid for. Now I was in a double panic. My purse had been stolen and I was a shoplifter! What if I got arrested? I had no ID to show because my purse had been stolen!

I continued toward the car, still discombobulated. The doors were locked, and I could see that my purse was not inside. I turned around and raced back to the front of the store, convinced that I must've somehow misplaced my purse in the basket area. Nope. Wrong. Purse wasn't there.

As I pushed the basket back into the store, a young woman stopped me. She looked really, really upset. With hands firmly planted on her hips, she said, "Ma'am...I believe you have my basket."

W–w–what? I looked down, and the basket contained the very same produce I'd put in my cart. The woman pointed off in the distance and said, "I see another basket over there with a purse in it. Is that yours?" She gave me a motherly look and said, "Ma'am, you really shouldn't leave your purse in your basket like that! Someone could steal it!"

It took about ten minutes for me to calm down once I got my purse and the right basket. I felt like the biggest goober in the world. Maybe you can relate. Maybe you've done something equally as goofy out of pure distraction. You didn't set out to make a spectacle of yourself, but that's what happened in the end. Distractions have a tendency to take us places we never meant to go. Today, why not ask the Lord to sharpen your focus? You're far less likely to wander off course (or out of the grocery store) when you're paying attention.

I will meditate on your precepts
and fix my eyes on your ways.
PSALM 119:15 ESV

Prayer

Lord, sometimes I set out to do one thing and end up doing something entirely different. I'm so easily distracted by things going on around me. I need Your help to stay focused, Father—not just today, but every day. Can You help me with that? Please? Amen.

Written in Buttercream

Writing in buttercream might come easily for some people, but not for me, especially since most of my cakes are tiered. (Ever tried writing on a wall with a bag of buttercream? It's pretty much the same concept.)

I recently took on a tiered graduation cake with writing on the side. Before I started writing, the cakes were spectacular with gorgeous piping. Then came the task of adding the writing. I hadn't left enough room for the words but tried to cram them in anyway. They came out crooked, huge, and impossible to read. I tried to fix it. No luck. Then I tried again, scraping away a bit of the maroon icing, which got all mixed up in the white cake icing. The whole section of the cake turned a mottled pinkish color and the icing was lumpy. Finally, in desperation, I pulled the tiered cake apart, completely scraped off all the icing on the top cake, made a new batch of buttercream, and started over. This time I wrote on the front of the cake before adding the colorful piping bits (something I should've thought of the first time around). It didn't look perfect but certainly turned out better than the first go-round.

Maybe you can relate. You're headed to a big event and need to look your best. You've planned it out in your head. You've added the right clothes and makeup. You've left room for accessories. Only one problem: You're not happy with the final product. You stare in the mirror and feel like gagging. You're not the picture of perfection you'd imagined you would be. The hair's not right, the makeup looks odd, the skirt doesn't fit properly, you don't have the right shoes to top off the ensemble.

The truth is, we're hard on ourselves. We want everything to be picture-perfect, but life just isn't like that. Sometimes the buttercream turns pink. Sometimes the blouse doesn't work with the slacks. Sometimes, despite your best attempts, that crazy hair refuses to be styled.

Relax! Be yourself. Go to the event anyway. Do your best to look at what's on the inside. (Have I mentioned that this cake had a yummy chocolate interior with mini chocolate chips and delicious homemade buttercream?) It might sound cliché, but it really is what's on the inside that matters.

Your beauty should not come from outward adornment, such as elaborate hairstyles and the wearing of gold jewelry or fine clothes. Rather, it should be that of your inner self, the unfading beauty of a gentle and quiet spirit, which is of great worth in God's sight.
1 PETER 3:3–4 NIV

Prayer

I'll be the first to admit it, Lord—I'm hard on myself. Sometimes I take myself too seriously or worry too much about what others will think. Thanks for the reminder that I need to relax and enjoy being myself. I'm made in Your image, after all. Amen.

Cream Cheese Soup

Note to self: never make two different kinds of icing in side-by-side mixers. It might just lead to catastrophe.

Things started well. I was making cream cheese icing in the mixing bowl on the right and white royal icing in the bowl on the left. The cream cheese icing was finished and resting in the bowl, ready to be used. Time to add the water to the meringue powder in the bowl on the left. I filled my half-cup measuring cup with water, reached over, and poured it...into the wrong bowl.

Instead of royal icing on the left, I ended up with cream cheese soup on the right.

Ugh.

Only one way to fix this: I had to add more powdered sugar to the cream cheese frosting. Only, the point of cream cheese icing is to add less-than-usual powdered sugar so that the tartness of the cream cheese come shining through. Would this wreck my chances? I had no other choice, so I poured in another cup of powdered sugar.

Still too soupy.

I added more powdered sugar.

Still not thick enough.

By the time I'd added enough sugar to stiffen up the cream cheese frosting, it was so sweet it made my cheeks hurt. I couldn't start over because I didn't have enough ingredients on hand, so I had to explain to my guest (a friend, not a customer) what had happened. She didn't seem to mind a bit, but I did! Sure, the frosting looked normal. But I knew the truth: water could never be as good or as rich as the right ingredients.

Maybe you know what it means to water down your faith. You've forgotten the power of the cross. You've fallen into the trap of caring more about social norms than Biblical truth. You just don't care as much as you used to about your walk with God. You've compromised.

It's not too late to stiffen up your faith and return to a solid walk with God. Maybe today is the day to do just that.

I know your works: you are neither cold nor hot.
Would that you were either cold or hot!
So, because you are lukewarm, and neither hot nor cold,
I will spit you out of my mouth.
REVELATION 3:15–16 ESV

Prayer

I don't want to be watered down, Lord. I don't want to be lukewarm. Today I recommit myself to You. Build my faith as I lean on You, my solid Rock. Amen.

That's Gnat Funny

A good friend commissioned me to bake a simple, textured, four-tiered wedding cake for her son. It came together easily.

Getting the cake set up at the venue turned out to be a bit more complicated. When I arrived, the entire wedding party gathered around me and watched as I stacked the four tiers. Nothing like having an audience in your face as you sweat your way through a cake assembly. No worries, though. It all came together beautifully. Later that evening, under balmy skies, the cake was transported to the outdoor reception area. Thank goodness, it arrived intact. I relaxed and enjoyed my time as a guest and never gave the cake another thought...until I realized how warm and sticky the weather was getting. Hopefully the buttercream wouldn't slide down the side of the cake. I walked to the cake table, which was near the lake, to give the front of the cake a solid once-over. The buttercream was glistening a bit but holding its own.

Then I happened to notice something on the back side of the cake. Tiny black dots covered the buttercream. I leaned in close and gasped when I realized the softened buttercream was covered in gnats. The warm, humid weather, combined with the cake's location near the lake, had offered an invitation to every gnat in the neighborhood. I called together a group of friends and asked them to stand guard by the cake in case the wedding coordinator decided to bring the bride and groom over to start the cutting process. Only one problem—my pals couldn't stop laughing.

The longer they stood there, the funnier the situation seemed to them. I ran to my car and fetched an offset spatula. Minutes later, with my friends still hovering around me, I scraped off gnat after gnat until the cake was servable.

Maybe you can relate to this story. Maybe you've worked hard to make everything in your life picture-perfect. Then something beyond your control comes along to mess up a perfectly good situation. It's a fiasco. God moves in with His spiritual spatula and, with one swoop, cleans up the mess. Everything is wiped clean.

Isn't it good to know that God is the ultimate fixer? What you can't do on your own, He's more than capable of handling for you. What a great God we serve!

If we are living in the light, as God is in the light,
then we have fellowship with each other,
and the blood of Jesus, His Son, cleanses us from all sin.
I JOHN 1:7 NLT

Prayer

Father, I confess I often find myself in messes beyond my control. And though I long to fix things, there are many times when I simply can't. Today I choose to trust You, the great Fixer. Use my messes for Your glory, I pray, Lord! Amen.

Daisy and the Pralines

My beagle, Daisy, can sniff out food a mile away. And trust me when I say she always manages to find the good stuff, even when I think I've hidden it.

Now, if you saw my chubby beagle you would say, "She's harmless. That pooch could never reach the table or countertop."

You would be wrong.

I found this out the hard way one holiday season. My friend had borrowed my kitchen to make pralines, a gift she planned to give her friends and loved ones. She left the candy to cool on the island and made a quick run to the grocery store to buy more ingredients. When she got back, most of the pralines were gone. The waxed paper was still there...but at least half of the candies had simply disappeared.

I arrived home shortly thereafter. We surveyed the scene and tried to figure out how this could have happened. Only a couple of days later, when I caught Daisy on the back of the sofa, ready to make a flying leap to the island, did I figure it out. My chubby beagle was an aerial artist.

Maybe you're a little bit like Daisy. You're tempted to do the wrong thing—eat that candy bar, gossip behind a friend's back, spend money you don't really have. You do your best to resist the temptation but then the urge accelerates and pulls you in, like a beagle to a praline. You just can't seem to help yourself. You climb to the top of the proverbial sofa and take a flying leap toward what you want.

If you're like Daisy, the consequences are swift and sure. Her temptation led to a very sick belly. There was a price to pay for giving in. There will be a price for you, too, which is why temptation is best avoided. Otherwise, you might just end up wishing you could turn back the clock for a second chance.

*No temptation has overtaken you
that is not common to man.
God is faithful, and he will not let you
be tempted beyond your ability,
but with the temptation he will also provide
the way of escape, that you may be able to endure it.*
I CORINTHIANS 10:13 ESV

Prayer

Father, it's so hard to resist temptation. I want to leap over the sofa and go for the gold. But I know there will be a price to pay, so please help me resist. I want to be diligent in my walk with You, so steer me away from the things that would hold me back, I pray. Amen.

Stick a Flower on It

My daughter and son-in-law were still grieving the loss of their daughter Evie when God blessed them with baby Isaac. About halfway into the pregnancy we started planning the baby shower. It was going to be a doozy, with over one hundred people in attendance. All of our friends and loved ones wanted to come out and bless this new child.

Everything was planned out perfectly, including the cake, which I had agreed to bake. The shower had a theme of bow ties and arrows, which I loved, but problems began even before I started baking. I was working with a finger injury, which made the process difficult. I began with the cookies, which were adorable. I was so happy to have them done. Thankfully, the cake came out looking terrific, too. I was so proud of my creations and couldn't wait to show them off the following day.

On the morning of the shower I prepared myself to lift the three-tiered cake and carry it to the car. My finger was really giving me fits, so I knew it would be a challenge. I managed to heft the cake into position and carry it outside, where the back of my SUV stood open. Whew! Made it!

At the very last minute, however, the whole thing tipped slightly, just enough to bump into my blouse. No worries. I could wash off the icing. I went ahead and situated the cake in the car, then gave it a closer look. Apparently, I'd done some damage to the beautiful buttercream rosettes when they hit my blouse. I ran back in the house, grabbed a spare bag of icing, and tried to fix it, only it just looked worse after the fact.

An idea hit me at once. I ran into my office and started rummaging through my craft supplies. There, in the middle of ribbons and glitter, I found a large silk flower, a perfect match to the cake. With no time for an alternate plan, I raced out to the car and stuck the flower on the front of the cake. I still laugh when I see photos of that cake. I knew what it was covering up underneath.

Maybe you can relate. Maybe you slap on a smile when there's really pain or bitterness underneath. Maybe you're afraid for people to see the truth because they'll find it ugly. The truth is, God can do business with all you're hiding if you'll let Him. He longs to do that even today.

Nothing is covered up that will not be revealed, or hidden that will not be known.
LUKE 12:2 ESV

Prayer

Lord, today I ask You to reveal all that is hidden just below the surface. I want to come clean with the things I've buried deep inside so that You can help me, Father. Start today, I pray. Amen.

Brittle Fondant

When I first started baking tiered cakes, I was pretty clueless but filled with zeal. A few months into my cake-baking journey, a good friend came to my house to teach me how to make homemade marshmallow fondant, a tasty alternative to the rubbery boxed stuff that most people despise. We had the best time, rolling out fun shapes and placing them on the cake. Forming the colorful claylike balls of marshmallowy fondant made me feel like a kid again.

A few weeks later, I made the decision to make another batch so that I could decorate my granddaughter's multitiered birthday cake. I'm still not sure where I went wrong. Maybe I added too much powdered sugar? Maybe I left the cutout pieces sitting out in the open air too long. Much to my horror, the fondant hardened like plastic. I had no choice—with no time left to lose, I had to put the decorative bits on the cake anyway. Instead of cutting into soft, pliable fondant at the party, little brittle pieces snapped off right and left. In happier news, it tasted yummy and no one got hurt.

I got to thinking about it after the fact. That brittle fondant reminded me a bit of myself. Over the years, I'd grown a little hard around the edges. Life's disappointments and pains had caused me to become somewhat brittle. Some days I snapped all over the place.

What about you? Can you relate? Are you pliable and flexible in the Potter's hands, or have life's cares gotten to you, dried you up? Have you become so set in your ways that you can't—or won't—bend? Careful!

Those sharp edges can do damage to others and even to you.

God longs for us to be workable in His hands, like clay for a potter. When we submit ourselves to the process, He can mold us into all He desires us to be.

"Go down to the potter's house,
and there I will give you My message."
So I went down to the potter's house,
and I saw him working at the wheel.
But the pot he was shaping from the clay was marred
in his hands; so the potter formed it into another pot,
shaping it as seemed best to him.
JEREMIAH 18:2-4 NIV

Prayer

Father, I submit myself to the molding process today. I will remain pliable in Your hands as You shape me into Your image. Amen.

A Smoky Lesson

I didn't mean to catch the oven on fire. In fact, I rarely mean to do any of the crazy things I do. But that particular Easter Sunday I'd baked up a feast for my family, a process that resulted in some overflow in the oven. No worries. I would deal with that later. We ate until our bellies were full, visited for a few hours, and then my guests left. I set my very gooey oven to self-clean mode and settled down to enjoy a show on TV.

A short while later, the smoke detectors went off. *Strange.* I turned around to discover smoke billowing in plumes from the closed oven door. *What in the world?* Seconds later, flames filled the inside of the oven. Through the glass on front, I watched them dance.

I jumped and ran to the oven but couldn't open it because it was locked tight for self-cleaning. Good thing, too, because if I'd managed to get that door open, the rush of oxygen would have resulted in more flames, likely causing a full-out house fire! (Thank you, Mr. Fireman, for sharing this information with me after the fact.)

Smoke flooded the room, making vision poor and breathing difficult. My poor mama. Well into the throes of Alzheimer's at this time, she was a nervous wreck. I had to walk her out to the backyard, away from the smoke, while I called 911.

Two fire trucks and seven firemen later, the house was cleared of smoke and we were finally able to come back inside. I was embarrassed, but at least we were safe.

I've thought about that evening many times since

then. We often stagger around in a fog, unable to see clearly. Our own mistakes prevent us from having the clarity we once had. Then Jesus, the ultimate fire fighter, enters the scene and blows away the fog so that we can start fresh.

What foggy situation are you facing? Ask the Lord to intervene and clear the air, that you might see clearly.

> *We don't yet see things clearly.*
> *We're squinting in a fog, peering through a mist.*
> *But it won't be long before the weather clears*
> *and the sun shines bright! We'll see it all then,*
> *see it all as clearly as God sees us,*
> *knowing Him directly just as He knows us!*
> I CORINTHIANS 13:12 THE MESSAGE

Prayer

Father, You've come to my rescue so many times. I'm so very grateful for the times You led me through foggy seasons. Clear my path today, I pray, that I may stick close to You. Amen.

A Pie for Mama

My mother passed away in the summer of 2017. The following Christmas, everyone gathered for our final holiday get-together at the house I had shared with her. (The house would sell shortly thereafter, so this was a bittersweet affair.)

I started fretting over Mama's chocolate pie weeks before Christmas. I knew that my kids and grandkids would expect it, especially this year. When Mama made it, perfectly creamed chocolate filling sat inside a beautifully baked shell. The whole thing was topped with exquisite meringue, light and fluffy. Yum. This delicious dessert held a place of honor at every holiday meal.

Only one problem...I can't bake a decent pie to save my life. Oh, I've made a few with store-bought crusts, but this year I decided to try my hand at Mama's recipe so that the family would be satisfied. Things started going awry when the crust shrank to about half its starting size. I tried again, but my next results weren't any better. To make matters worse, my filling didn't thicken properly, and with the rest of Christmas dinner to cook, I never made it to the meringue. In the end, the whole thing went into the trash. There would be no chocolate pie for Christmas.

My family was very understanding. They ate the cookies, cakes, and store-bought pies. No one grumbled (much) about the missing pie. I decided to take Mama's favorite pie dish and set it at the end of our dining room table, to represent her. I hated to make it an empty dish, but what else could I do?

Maybe you can relate to the loss of a loved one. Who are you thinking of today? Take some time to reflect on the memories and then do something special in your loved one's honor today. No matter how it turns out, the memories will be just as sweet.

> *So also you have sorrow now,*
> *but I will see you again,*
> *and your hearts will rejoice,*
> *and no one will take your joy from you.*
> JOHN 16:22 ESV

Prayer

Lord, I miss my loved ones who've gone before me, but I know they are safe in Your care. I can't wait to be reunited in heaven. (Can we get together for a bake-a-thon in my mansion?) Until then, I will honor the one I love in all I say and do. Amen.

Shirley Ann's Chocolate Pie

INGREDIENTS

- 3 egg yolks
- 1 cup sugar
- ¼ cup cornstarch
- 2 tablespoons cocoa powder
- Dash salt
- 2½ cups milk
- 1 teaspoon vanilla
- 3 tablespoons butter

INSTRUCTIONS

Beat egg yolks and set aside.

In a microwavable bowl, combine sugar, cornstarch, cocoa powder, and salt. Whisk until incorporated and lump-free. Slowly pour in milk, continually stirring.

Microwave in 1-minute increments, stirring between each one. Mixture should be thickened at about the 7-minute mark.

Remove chocolate mixture from microwave and slowly add egg yolks. Whisk rapidly to incorporate. Stir in vanilla and butter and mix well, then pour into baked pie crust. Cool before serving.

Meringue Recipe

INGREDIENTS

- 4 egg whites
- 1 cup hot water
- 6 tablespoons sugar
- 1 tablespoon cornstarch

INSTRUCTIONS

Whip egg whites until they form a soft peak. Set aside. Cook water, sugar, and cornstarch until thick. Add quickly to egg whites while beating for 30 seconds. Spoon onto pie. Bake at 350°F until golden.

For added zing, top with coconut, shaved chocolate, or lemon zest before serving.

Stabilized Whipped Cream Frosting

INGREDIENTS

- 1 large container heavy whipping cream
- ¼ cup sugar
- 1 package instant pudding (any flavor you like)

INSTRUCTIONS

Whip the cream to soft peaks. Add ¼ cup sugar, then the full box of instant pudding. Mix until the whipped cream takes on a creamy consistency.

For additional choices, choose from the following pudding flavors:

- Lemon
- Vanilla
- Chocolate
- Butterscotch
- Banana cream
- White chocolate

These stabilized whipped creams are luscious when used with fruits.

Janice's Homemade Marshmallow Fondant

INGREDIENTS

- 1 bag mini marshmallows
- 2 tablespoons water
- 1 tablespoon white Karo syrup (optional)
- 1 teaspoon almond extract
- 1 tablespoon vanilla extract
- 6-8 cups of powdered sugar (add one cup at a time until it reaches a doughlike consistency)
- 2 tablespoons of shortening (to coat the fondant)

BEFORE YOU BEGIN

Spray the following with nonstick spray: a large plastic microwavable bowl, a large spoon, stand mixer bowl, and hook attachment.

ADD TO BOWL

- Full bag of marshmallows
- 2 tablespoons water

INSTRUCTIONS

Microwave for 1 minute, then stir. Microwave again for 30 seconds (or until marshmallows are melted).

When the marshmallows are done, stir well with spoon and pour into stand mixer bowl (with hook attachment). Add a tablespoon of white Karo syrup, a teaspoon of almond extract, and a tablespoon of vanilla extract. Slowly add powdered sugar, 1 cup at a time, until fondant texture reaches a doughlike consistency. Remove from bowl, coat in shortening, and store in a sealed plastic bag in a dark place for 24 hours (to cure) before using. (If you use it right away, it will tear.) Use Americolor gels to color.

NOTE: If you don't have a stand mixer, you can knead the fondant by hand. Make sure your prep area has a lot of powdered sugar on hand so that you can incorporate it into the marshmallow liquid as you work.

Cake Tips

Oh, how I love cake: white, chocolate, Italian cream, lemon raspberry, zebra-striped, turtle, Oreo... you name it, I love it. Cover it in my homemade cream cheese buttercream and/or my homemade fondant and...yum!

Here's a little secret, for those who are wondering: Many of my cakes start with a boxed mix, but I always add to the mix to make the finished product extra-tasty. For instance, a wedding cake (or any other white cake, for that matter) will call for the addition of both vanilla and almond extracts. I use only egg whites in white cakes, to keep the cakes as white as possible. My chocolate cakes often call for the substitution of butter for oil, etc.

Here are some great cake-baking tips:

- First, both grease and flour your pans. A light sprinkling of flour will do it.

- Second, if you're baking a large cake, set the temperature about 10 degrees lower and cook a few extra minutes.

- Third, completely cool your cakes before decorating. Once they reach room temperature, turn them out of the pans to cool and then put them in the fridge to firm up before adding the frosting. Many people freeze their cakes days ahead and work with them frozen or semithawed.

- Fourth, sift all dry ingredients, even boxed mixes. You don't want lumps in your cake.

- Finally...relax! What's the worst that can happen, anyway? You botch a cake and end up eating it yourself!

Tiered Cakes

If you plan to make a tiered cake, you'll need several things in advance. My go-to list includes the following:

1. A turntable

2. A cake "dome" (foil-covered, thick board) for the bottom cake tier to sit on. I often make my own out of cake rounds/boards and foil baker's wrap. It needs to be strong enough to hold the weight of the entire cake.

3. Speaking of cake rounds, you'll need them in the exact sizes of each tier's cakes.

4. Boba/milkshake straws (*or* dowels)

5. An offset spatula

How to Tier

Let's pretend we're making a typical three-tiered cake (birthday, wedding, or otherwise). Imagine that each tier has three layers of cake in your favorite flavor.

BOTTOM TIER

Place your cake dome on the turntable. Level off your largest three cakes (bottom tier cakes) and begin the process of stacking and filling them. When you're done with the stacking process, dirty-ice the cake (add a thin crumb coat of frosting) and put it into the fridge for at least ten minutes. When it's chilled, remove from the fridge and add your support straws (or dowels). How many you add will depend on the number of tiers above this one and the overall weight of the cake. If I'm doing a ten-inch bottom cake, I'll usually add seven or eight bubble-tea straws to the bottom tier. Once the support rods are added, ice and decorate your cake.

MIDDLE TIER

Using a cake round in the same size as the cakes, stack and fill, then dirty-ice. Once it's chilled, add the supports. You won't need as many for this layer. For a typical eight-inch middle tier, I'll add five or six straws. Once the supports are added, frost and decorate the cake, then set it on top of the bottom tier. (You're almost there!)

TOP TIER

Repeat the process you used on the middle tier, this time using a smaller cake board. Depending on the stability of this top tier, you might get away with not using any support straws or dowels.

Once your cake is assembled, make sure everything is level. For added support, run a longer dowel down through the center of all three cakes. (If you do this, you'll have to leave a hole in the center of each board first. Many cake boards now come with holes in them for this very purpose.) Now it's time to add your final decorations. If you've got ribbons or flowers, this is the time to add them. If you're planning to "trim out" the layers (using your piping tips), it will add the finishing touches.

NOTE: If you're transporting a tiered cake, you must have a level surface in your vehicle. Also, it's nearly impossible to find a box large enough to fit a tiered cake. I usually transport mine unboxed. If I'm traveling to a wedding with a four-tiered cake, I'll wait to assemble the cake until I arrive.

There you have it, friends! A tiered cake isn't as intimidating as you once thought!

Life happens.
Baking helps.

ANONYMOUS

Bake the World a Better Place

INTRODUCTION

Have you ever thought about why people love baked goods so much? They always seem to bring a smile to the faces of their recipients. Some would even say they could bring about world peace. Sure, they're sweet and delectable. And, yes, they look beautiful and tempting as you pass them off to their intended recipients. But perhaps there's more to this phenomenon than meets the eye.

When you give someone a cake, cookies, bread, or a pie, you're giving them your time, efforts, and talent. You're saying, "You were worth spending a few hours in the kitchen. You matter to me." The one receiving your gift understands all of this without saying a word. She also understands that your offering is meant to soothe whatever trouble she's facing and ease whatever struggle she's going through. It's an offering of love and hope all wrapped up in a sugary coating.

Whether you've got a cranky neighbor, a political foe, or an angry boss, baked goods can serve to pacify and mend. Hand someone a cookie and the words "I forgive you" are spoken. Give her a slice of cake and the words "Can we just forget about that little quarrel we had?" rush out.

At this very moment, all around the globe, people

are bringing about world peace by baking for others. They're pulling hot loaves of bread from the oven, stacking crispy peanut butter cookies onto a platter, or frosting cakes with great care. They're prepping boxes for delivery and writing heartfelt notes to accompany their gift.

Baked goods really can bring about peace on earth, one sweet treat at a time. They remind us that people were never meant to do life alone. They say to the one on the receiving end: "I'm right here with you. I can see what you're going through, and I want to help." More than anything, they offer slivers of hope to people in tough places.

Merging and Converging

There's a particular technique used by cookie artists that has beautiful (and often unexpected) results. They call it "wet on wet." The cookie is covered in one color of royal icing, and then drops of a second color are added while the first is still wet. The colors merge and converge, creating a single layer of icing—completely flush. Best of all, you can take a toothpick and drag it through the wet colors, creating all sorts of fascinating designs—hearts, cable knitting, and so on. The possibilities are endless and oh so colorful!

I love the merge-and-converge technique. I use it all the time to create polka dots, hearts, winter sweater cookies, and fun psychedelic color combinations. I particularly enjoy using this technique on surfboard cookies. Cool, dude! Hang ten!

The most amazing part of the process is watching how one color moves over and allows room for the other. Fascinating! It accommodates. It doesn't fight for space. It doesn't even cause the second color to fade or blur. It simply shifts position as the weight of the second color arrives on the scene. How blissful, to see the outcome of this generosity as the final product is revealed.

Isn't this an amazing life lesson for us, as well? God calls us to live in unity, to accommodate, to love others (often at the expense of our own comfort). Like that initial round of icing, we're called to move over and make room for the next guy. Sometimes we do so willingly; other times we refuse to budge. But God is honored when we merge and converge.

When we choose to prefer others over ourselves, the result can be beautiful. And sweet! Others will see the body of Christ as giving, loving, and generous... exactly who He has called us to be.

> *Be kindly affectioned one to another*
> *with brotherly love;*
> *in honour preferring one another.*
> ROMANS 12:10 KJV

Prayer

Lord, I'll admit, it's not always easy to prefer others or to put their wants, wishes, or needs above my own. But You've called me to do so, Father! I want to be accommodating. After all, You've accommodated me so many times and in so many ways. Have I thanked You for that, Lord? Today I choose to do so. Praise You for all You've done for me! Amen.

Jenna Eats the Air

There's nothing more delightful than a child who loves to watch her grandma bake. So when Jenna (my five-year-old granddaughter who has dealt with health issues all her life) spent the day with me, I had to get her in the kitchen.

Jenna loves to pull up a barstool and get right next to my stand mixer. She also loves to help put the ingredients in the bowl—something that has led to more than one fiasco, but I don't mind. Mostly she loves it when I work with powdered sugar because it "poofs."

Don't know what "poofing" is? It's that moment when you add powdered sugar and the blades of the mixer send it poofing into the air and all over the countertop. If you're not careful (and I never claimed to be) you can end up with a mess all over the place. (I refer back to my story about the dog who got a powdered-sugar shower.)

Jenna loves the poof. She waits in expectation, hoping a fog of white will rise from the bowl. One particular day I turned around to discover her licking the air above the mixer. Sure enough, she was catching poofs of powdered sugar on her tongue. She giggled and repeated the action, each time getting a bit more sweetness. The giggles went on and on as she lapped at the mist.

I couldn't help but watch in pure delight as she ate the air. This precious girl, who had been through so much, found such joy in something incredibly simple. She was completely mesmerized.

Isn't that how God longs for each of us to be? No matter what we're going through, He longs for us to delight in Him, to find joy in every little thing. It's those moments—those precious, holy moments—that He is at work in our hearts, bringing joy into even the darkest situations.

What are you struggling with today? Take a moment. Wait for it. A "poof" is coming. The Holy Spirit is about to amaze and delight you right in the middle of your struggle.

> *The LORD your God is in your midst,*
> *a mighty one who will save;*
> *he will rejoice over you with gladness;*
> *he will quiet you by his love;*
> *he will exult over you with loud singing.*
> ZEPHANIAH 3:17 ESV

Prayer

Father, I take delight in You! I will look for those special moments, those "poofs" from You. I'll be ready and waiting to lap up Your goodness, Lord. Thank You for interrupting our lives with joy-filled encounters. I'm so grateful. Amen.

Ooh-La-La

My granddaughter Peyton is in love with all things Paris. In fact, we've already planned a trip to France for her thirteenth birthday. I'm putting away a little money every month to make that dream a reality for her.

When it came time to plan Peyton's 9th birthday party, the Paris theme was a given. Her mother entrusted all of the baking (and much of the decorating) to me, since I love themed parties.

I found the perfect cupcake tower online—one shaped like the Eiffel tower. And the best possible cupcake liners—black-and-white-striped. I planned to bake yummy cupcakes and decorate them in soft pink. With the ideal color combo, we were halfway to Paris already.

After a bit of searching, I found a candy mold shaped like the Eiffel Tower as well, so I purchased that, melted chocolate, colored it soft pink, and poured it into the molds. Voilà! I now had the perfect toppers to go on the pink, black, and white cupcakes.

Of course, we also had to locate paper products to go with this ensemble. No problem! The Internet provided me lots of options in our color scheme. By the time all was said and done, I'd completely transformed my dining room into a Parisian masterpiece. Peyton was blown away and so were her friends, as they enjoyed a European tea complete with cupcakes and other sweet treats.

This might sound like a lot of work to go to for a ten-year-old. Some might even think it extravagant. But I loved every second of it. Nothing (and I do mean nothing) brings me greater pleasure than creating fun memories for the little ones in my life. To pour out blessings on the ones I love is one of the key highlights of my life.

I have to believe that God feels the same way about us. It must surely bring Him great joy to shower unexpected blessings on us. Oh, the thought and planning that must go into some of His ventures! He knows our likes, our dislikes, our personalities, our dreams. And He cares about it all, down to the tiniest detail.

As much as Peyton appreciated her grandmother's attention to detail, I'm even more blown away by God's great blessings in my life. What an adventure, to see where He will take me next! (Paris, anyone?)

You will eat the fruit of your labor;
blessings and prosperity will be yours.
PSALM 128:2 NIV

Prayer

Lord, I don't know what unexpected blessings You have in store, but I can't wait to discover them! I feel like a kid again, Father, as I watch (with great wonder) all that You're doing in my life. I'm as grateful as a kid at a birthday party. Thank You for lavishing me with Your love. Amen.

Never Trust a Groomsman

My piping skills are moderate at best. So when a friend asked for an intricately detailed wedding cake for her daughter—one loaded with black piping on an all-white cake—I hesitated.

Okay, I more than hesitated...I panicked.

Then I calmed down and worked on my piping skills. I somehow managed to pull off a lovely four-tiered beauty with pretty black piping and gorgeous handmade red fondant roses. Woo-hoo!

Transporting cakes is never easy, but I wasn't terribly worried about this one. I just needed to make sure someone strong and capable helped me lift the cake when I arrived at the church because it was a bit too heavy for me to lift on my own.

Never fear! Groomsman to the rescue! The burly fellow was happy to be of service...so happy, in fact, that he didn't wait for instructions. He reached over to grab the cake base and promptly ran his hand through the bottom tier of the cake, destroying all my beautiful piping and leaving a gaping hole in the cake.

I've never wanted to punch a groomsman before, but that one nearly got a wallop! Instead of panicking, I managed a smile and told him not to worry, that I would fix it. And fix it I did! Before the bride and groom ever laid eyes on their beautiful four-tiered wonder, I'd patched the hole and repiped the design on top. (Yay for remembering to bring extra frosting and piping gel!)

Maybe you can relate to this story. Maybe you've spent hours, days, weeks working on a project, only to have someone else destroy it. Maybe your boss couldn't be bothered to watch your presentation or listen to your carefully-thought-out ideas. Maybe you poured your energies into a friendship or romantic relationship, only to watch someone tear it apart. Maybe the dog ate your homework.

The truth is, we all know what it feels like to be sabotaged (whether inadvertently or otherwise). The real question is, How are we, as followers of Christ, supposed to respond when our work/situation seems to be ruined? Whether we are victims of deliberate sabotage or someone's inadvertent mistake, our reaction has to be the same: Instead of knee-jerking, we've got to take a deep breath and then respond as Christ would respond. Instead of a wallop, offer grace.

See to it that no one falls short of the grace of God and that no bitter root grows up to cause trouble and defile many.
HEBREWS 12:15 NIV

Prayer

Lord, I hate the sting of sabotage! I've felt it from those who wished to do me wrong and even from those who've accidentally or inadvertently hurt me. Today I choose to forgive those who've left gaping holes. I take out that emergency kit (Your Word) and patch the broken places. Thank You, Father, for showing me that I can recover, once I extend grace and forgiveness. Amen.

Christmas Trees to Remember

I was asked to come up with a baking craft for twenty to thirty women for an event at my church. I racked my brain for ideas.

Finally, it hit me. I could bake mini cupcakes, whip up bags and bags of frosting, and purchase Styrofoam "trees." The goal? The ladies could work together to toothpick the unfrosted cupcakes to the foam trees, then pipe on green frosting to create gorgeous edible Christmas trees. At that point, we could add red and gold candies to serve as ornaments. Together, we would pull off the perfect themed treat.

I baked what felt like a zillion cupcakes. And though my math skills aren't stellar, I was sure I'd prepared enough to cover the Styrofoam trees.

Wrong.

On the night of the event, the ladies worked meticulously to pin the cupcakes to their bases, but I forgot to tell them to space them out a bit. Each team used up all of their cupcakes before they reached the top of the tree. Ugh. Now what? I had a bit of frosting left over, so I gave the ladies instructions to add as much as they could to the top of the Styrofoam cone to cover our mess.

I got the bright idea to fasten a large Christmas bow on the top of each tree, which made it (almost) impossible to see the missing cupcakes underneath.

Whew!

Don't you love it when you work with a team like that? There's something so fun about accomplishing tasks with those you love. Of course, group efforts don't always come together seamlessly (especially when the leader's math skills leave something to be desired), but teamwork is still a blast.

God designed us to work like that—with others who can fill in the gaps where we leave off. When we operate in unity, we can accomplish much for the kingdom of God! Don't believe me? Just try building cupcake trees with your friends!

Two are better than one, because they have a good reward
for their toil. For if they fall, one will lift up his fellow.
But woe to him who is alone when he falls and has not
another to lift him up! Again, if two lie together,
they keep warm, but how can one keep warm alone?
And though a man might prevail against one
who is alone, two will withstand him—
a threefold cord is not quickly broken.
ECCLESIASTES 4:9-12 ESV

Prayer

Lord, thank You for the women in my life. I'm grateful for the times You've allowed me to work alongside them—whether it's in the church, on the job, or in my neighborhood. I love the camaraderie, and I enjoy learning from those more skilled than I am. I'm so grateful, Father. Amen.

Taste and See

I love oatmeal-Craisin cookies. I love them for breakfast, for a snack, or for dessert. I love them with pecans or with walnuts. I love them hot from the oven or warmed-over a day later. I love them with coffee, tea, or a big glass of milk. I simply love these cookies. I love them so much that I recently decided to have a couple for breakfast. Because it was a perfectly lovely day, I decided to take the cookies and a cup of coffee out onto the back porch, where I settled in at the patio table.

Off in the distance, morning birds sang their joyful song. A lizard climbed up the wooden fence post. Blue skies hovered over me, cloudless and beautiful. A delicious breeze blew over me as I reached to take a little nibble. All was well with the world.

Then the unthinkable happened. From the patio below, my beagle, Daisy Mae, bounded onto an empty chair and then leaped onto the table. She sat down directly across from me and stared me down while I ate said cookie. I told her, "Scoot!" I told her, "Shoo!" I told her (very sternly), "Daisy Mae, get down from this table right away, or you'll be in big, big trouble!" She refused to budge. She zeroed in on that cookie and wasn't moving until I gave her a nibble.

Now, I'd like to say I resisted. I'd love to tell you that I scolded her, removed her from the table, and made her go back into the house while I ate. That's what a proper dog owner would do. But that's not what happened. Being the sucker that I am, I gave that ornery hound dog a little nibble of the delicious treat. Or two. Or maybe three.

As I watched Daisy staring with such longing, I couldn't help but think of my relationship with the Lord. I need to long for Him in the same way Daisy Mae longed for that cookie. I need to be willing to leap tall buildings (symbolically speaking) to spend time in His presence. There, in that precious place, He will bring peace as no one else can. He'll never say, "Shoo!" He'll never say, "You're in big, big trouble." Instead, He will welcome me with open arms and give me nibble after nibble of His sweetness and love. Now that's a tasty treat!

Taste and see
that the LORD is good;
blessed is the one
who takes refuge in Him.
PSALM 34:8 NIV

Prayer

Lord, thank You for the reminder that You are drawing me even now. The aroma of Your goodness, Your kindness, Your love is so tantalizing that I can't help but quit everything I'm doing, leap into Your presence, and spend quality time with You. Praise You, Father. Amen.

A Powdered-Sugar Mountain

Oh, the looks I get when I shop for ingredients. You just haven't lived until you've filled your cart with a dozen bags of powdered sugar, twenty pounds of flour, twenty-five pounds of sugar, eight pounds of butter, and multiple cartons of eggs. And don't even get me started on the extra ingredients—pecans and coconut for my German chocolate cake frosting or jars and jars of peanut butter for my delectable peanut butter cookies. My shopping cart overfloweth!

Every time I do what I call "big shopping," I end up at a register with a clerk who loves to chat about baking. Before the transaction has ended, I'm pulling out my phone and showing pictures of my latest baking efforts. This, of course, leads to a conversation from said clerk about a time he or she tried to bake a cake or flopped at a batch of cookies. I love these conversations so much because for that moment, nothing else in the world matters. The person standing across from me isn't on task anymore. I'm not stressed about shopping. We're just two new friends, talking about cakes, cupcakes, and cookies.

Baking is the great unifier, isn't it? You can go anywhere across this great globe, glance in the shopping cart of a baker, and feel right at home. When you're talking about that latest cake or cookie project, you're not wondering if the person on the other end of the conversation has the same political ideologies. You don't notice or care if he's tall, short, skinny, fluffy. You're not paying attention to dialects or skin color. All that matters is your common interest... baking.

Don't you wish life were always like that? What if we all put away our differences and focused on the things we have in common? Jesus is the greatest unifier of all. He can take a world full of very different people and merge them into one big, happy family.

There is neither Jew nor Greek,
there is neither slave nor free,
there is no male and female,
for you are all one in Christ Jesus.
GALATIANS 3:28 ESV

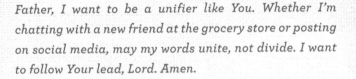
Prayer

Father, I want to be a unifier like You. Whether I'm
chatting with a new friend at the grocery store or posting
on social media, may my words unite, not divide. I want
to follow Your lead, Lord. Amen.

Pretty Please, with Sugar on Top

I'm so glad God hasn't called me to a life of full-time customer service. I'm not sure I would excel at it, as I learned with one particularly difficult baking customer. She came to me with her mind made up. She wanted what she wanted and she wanted it at her price. And on her timetable. She also wanted me to do something I'd never been asked to do before—provide her with a detailed sketch of the cake before making it. This I had to do based on her overly intricate details/ suggestions.

Now, I'm no artist. Well, not on paper, anyway. But I managed to come up with a sketch she approved of. I worked hard on it, coloring in the various tiers of the cowgirl cake in pinks, teals, browns, and whites. Talk about details. Whew. I still quiver, just thinking about how different each tier was from the others. In the end, she loved the design. I did, too.

I worked so hard on that cake. It looked adorable.

Well, all but one part. I tried to construct a little cowgirl boot for the top of the cake out of fondant. I should've gone with cereal treats (lighter in weight) because the boot refused to hold its shape. By the time my customer arrived to pick up the cake, cupcakes, and cookies, the little boot looked short and chubby at best.

Only, for whatever reason, my customer didn't seem to notice or care. I made profuse apologies and suggested she pull off the boot entirely, but she left it in place, proclaiming the whole order to be terrific.

People are funny, aren't they? I suspect she responded with such kindness because I'd gone out of my way to give her everything she'd asked for during the ordering process. I guess it's true what they say: "What goes around, comes around."

God shares this same principle in His Word: *Do unto others as you would have others do to you.* When we pour ourselves out on behalf of other people, we always receive blessings in response. Our generosity will never fail to result in blessing.

Sure, tough people will come and go. Not everyone will be easy to work with. But, in the end, treating people the way we long to be treated will be a true reflection of Christ and (might) win that person over.

Do to others as you would
have them do to you.
LUKE 6:31 NIV

Prayer

Father, I'll admit I don't always like to go out of my way for others. Sometimes I wish people would just lower their expectations or be less demanding. But You've called me to excellence, Father, so I will go on treating them as I would hope to be treated, even when those demands seem a bit much! You'll honor my diligence, I know, Lord. Thank You for that! Amen.

It's Cake o'Clock

I don't know why God wired me the way He did. So many things about me are different. Take, for instance, my body clock. It doesn't seem to match others', not even close. While the rest of the world snoozes, I'm wide awake in my kitchen, hand-painting cookies or baking wedding cakes. While they're halfway through their sleep cycle, I'm finally getting around to washing the dishes that piled up in my sink while baking. Even when I tumble into bed, I usually take a sneak peek at the Internet to learn more about buttercream techniques or cookie designs. There, in that quiet place, I strategize my next project. And the one after that. And the one after that.

I'm not sure why I work better in the late hours, but I do. I'm up and running while the rest of the world dozes. (Take it up with the Almighty, folks! He designed me this way.) It's nothing for me to start a project before noon and still be working at two or three in the morning. I'd like to think I do my best work after normal people go to bed. Of course, this also means that I won't be waking up with the chickens. You'll find me snoozing well past the time when others are headed out to work. I used to feel guilty about this, but no more! Now I give my body the time it needs to recover, no matter when I go to sleep.

God designed each of us differently, and He did so on purpose. The world would be incredibly boring if we all had everything in common. Maybe you're a morning person, up before dawn. Or maybe you crash every afternoon, ready for a nap. Who cares? Let that beautifully designed body of yours function as it was intended to, and don't worry about what others might think. Studies have shown that you get more work done during your creative peak time, so learn to love the body clock God gave you.

> *I praise you, for I am fearfully*
> *and wonderfully made.*
> *Wonderful are your works;*
> *my soul knows it very well.*
> PSALM 139:14 ESV

Prayer

Lord, I don't mind that I'm different from others; that doesn't bug me. I kind of like it, in fact. Who cares if my body clock is a little cuckoo? I want to stay faithful to how You designed me. Show me how to take care of myself while I do that, I pray. Amen.

Bake Someone Happy

I received the news midmorning that a good friend had been badly injured. While working on his ranch, a bizarre accident caused him to almost lose a finger. Before I could ask, "What happened?" he was in surgery. We all prayed the surgeon could save the finger (particularly since this friend happened to be the bass player at our church and depended on his fingers to lead worship).

I knew right away what needed to be done. My friend's favorite cake in the world was Italian cream cake. So, I pulled out my mixing bowls and got busy. By the time he was post-op, I had the pans in the oven. By the time he arrived home later that night, I was on my way with the cake.

What really made it special, though, was the decoration. I rolled out flesh-colored fondant, shaped it into a hand, placed it on the cake, then "bandaged up" one of the fingers. I even added red food coloring for blood. I piped the words "Give him a hand, folks!" onto the cake.

No, I don't have a morbid sense of humor...but my friend does. I knew he would get a kick out of it. And get a kick out of it he did! He still talks about that cake to this day. It lifted his spirits more than any card could have done. He realized how much I cared, and he never forgot it.

When you know someone really well, you know how to lift his spirits. Maybe you've got a friend or loved one who's going through a particularly tough time right now. Maybe she's dealing with the loss of a child or he's going through a divorce. If you want to make a lasting impact, pull out your mixing bowls and get busy. Put together a special treat to let that person know she is thought of, loved, and prayed for. Your love offering will go a long way in helping your friend recover.

One gives freely,
yet grows all the richer;
another withholds
what he should give,
and only suffers want.
Whoever brings blessing
will be enriched,
and one who waters
will himself be watered.
PROVERBS 11:24–25 ESV

Prayer

Lord, I want to be a blessing to others, especially those who are going through tough times. Please show me how I can reach out to others and impact their lives for the better, I pray. Amen.

Cherry Blossoms
(AN ADOPTION STORY)

If you were to ask my family, they would say that I "collect" people who need a mom. My house is always overflowing with young women in need of a mother figure. My youngest is adopted, but she's as much a part of our clan as my other three daughters.

Because I've always believed in the concept of adoption, I was tickled to hear that a good friend was planning to adopt two special-needs kiddos from China. I couldn't wait to see how God brought their plans to fruition. She and her husband flew to China, did the required paperwork, and brought those adorable kiddos (both toddlers) back to Texas. I watched it all firsthand, thanks to social media.

Several close friends decided to throw a baby shower for the family. Because the kids were from Asia, I thought a cherry blossom–themed tree was in order. Instead of the usual pink blossoms, I did both pink and blue to represent both boy and girl. I'm pretty sure I even colored the inside of the cake in pink, blue, and white. I topped the whole thing off with little owl cookies, who sat perched atop the tree. Perfect!

As I looked across the sea of faces on the day of the shower, I saw people who were all unique, different. Different nationalities. Different styles of dress. Different mannerisms. Different hairstyles. Different churches. Different personalities. Different desires. Different dreams. There, in that one room, we represented multiple nations.

Isn't it fun to realize that God sees us all as one big happy family? When He looks at us, He doesn't see differences. He sees His body. Just like those two precious children, we've been adopted into a family so vast, so eclectic, that we can't wrap our minds around it. And we are loved...every single one of us, with a love so passionate, so deep, that our Father crossed miles to make us His very own.

A father to the fatherless,
a defender of widows,
is God in His holy dwelling.
God sets the lonely in families,
He leads out the prisoners with singing.
PSALM 68:5–6 NIV

Prayer

Father, thank You for adopting me. Like my good friends, You crossed oceans to claim me. You wouldn't rest until I was Your own. I'm so glad to be Your kid, Lord! Amen.

Faith to Believe

It rarely happens that I have no words, but when a good friend was diagnosed with lymphoma, all I could say was, "I'm so sorry. I'm praying." It just didn't seem possible. But I knew we would find our answer in prayer, so pray I did! I joined a large group of prayer warriors who met online regularly to pray for this wonderful gentleman. We stormed the gates of heaven with each new obstacle he met. Our key word was "Believe!" And when he finally received word about eighteen months later that he was in remission, we celebrated together.

My friend's daughter decided to host a "Believe" party so that we could all come together and celebrate in person. I was asked to bake the cake and cookies. Of course I obliged. I was so excited about the project... until I looked up the color for the lymphoma ribbon and realized it was lime green. How could I make a lime green cake for a grown man who'd just come through something so serious? It seemed almost irreverent. This wasn't a kid's birthday party, after all!

In the end, I made one of the most delightful cakes I'd ever baked. A beautiful three-tiered wonder, it stood as tall and as magnificent as a wedding cake. Each tier was unique and lovely. The bottom tier was covered in lime rosettes; the upper layers added elements of white and teal with the "Believe" theme spelled out in fondant. On the very front of the center tier I placed a fondant lymphoma ribbon. Perfection! Everyone oohed and aahed over that cake. We were already in a jubilant frame of mine, and that lighthearted cake served to keep things joyful.

And why not? We had seen our friend through cancer. This was no time for mourning!

What about you? Are you walking a friend through cancer or another tough illness? May your faith grow stronger with each passing day, that you might stand in the gap for your friend as you believe for the best possible outcome.

> *Without faith*
> *it is impossible to please him,*
> *for whoever would draw near*
> *to God must believe*
> *that he exists and that*
> *he rewards those who seek him.*
> HEBREWS 11:6 ESV

Prayer

Father, I want to stand in the gap for my friends and loved ones who are hurting. Show me how to pray specifically, Lord. Give me the faith to believe, even for the impossible. With You, all things are possible. May I never forget. Amen.

Oatmeal-Craisin Pecan Cookies
(DOUBLE BATCH)

CREAM
- 1 cup butter

ADD AND CREAM WELL
- 1 cup packed brown sugar
- 1 cup granulated sugar

COMBINE AND BEAT IN UNTIL SMOOTH
- 2 eggs
- 2 teaspoons vanilla extract

SIFT TOGETHER AND ADD TO THE ABOVE INGREDIENTS
- 2 cups sifted all-purpose flour
- 1 teaspoon baking soda
- 1 teaspoon salt

WHEN BEATEN SMOOTH, ADD
- 3 cups uncooked quick oats

ADD
- 1 cup Craisins
- 1 cup chopped pecans

BEAT WELL.

Drop cookies 2 inches apart on a cookie sheet and bake 10–12 minutes at 350°F.

Peanut Butter Cookies

MIX TOGETHER
- ½ cup butter
- ½ cup shortening
- 1 cup packed brown sugar
- 1 cup granulated sugar
-

ADD
- 2 eggs
- 2 cups peanut butter
- ½ teaspoon salt
- 1 teaspoon baking soda
- 1 teaspoon vanilla extract

SIFT AND ADD
- 2½–3 cups all-purpose flour

Scoop into balls and use fork to indent with crosshatch pattern.

Bake on parchment paper–covered cookie sheet at 375°F for 11 minutes.

When the cookies are fresh from the oven, I like to sprinkle sugar on them.

NOTE: The original recipe called for 1 cup butter or shortening and I've always used butter (for the taste). I decided to do half and half, and oh my goodness! I still got the flavor of the butter but the fluffiness created by the shortening. The amount of flour can vary, depending on how you like it. I usually end up with about 2¾ cups.

ADDITIONAL NOTE: Add mini chocolate chips to the recipe for a fun variation.

German Chocolate Cake Cookies

If you love German chocolate cake but want it in cookie form, do I have a treat for you! You'll love these sweeter-than-coconut sandwich cookies stuffed with coconut pecan frosting!

PREHEAT OVEN TO 350°F.

MIX TOGETHER

- 1 box German chocolate cake
- ⅓ cup vegetable oil
- 2 eggs

WHEN THOROUGHLY MIXED, ADD

- ⅓ cup chopped pecans
- ¼ cup flaked coconut

As soon as the batter/dough is mixed, scoop into 1-inch balls and place on a parchment paper–lined cookie sheet. Bake for 11–15 minutes (depending on your oven).

MEANWHILE, IN A SAUCEPAN ON THE STOVETOP, MIX TOGETHER

- 6 ounces (½ can) evaporated milk
- ¾ cup granulated sugar
- 6 tablespoons butter
- 3 egg yolks, lightly whipped

Heat the evaporated milk, sugar, butter, and egg yolks in a heavy 3-qt. saucepan (medium heat). Don't stop stirring! Cook about 3 or 4 minutes. You'll know you're at the right point when the butter melts and the sugar is fully dissolved. Now, brace yourself! Time for a workout! Lower the heat and keep cooking (stirring nonstop) for 12–14 minutes or until mixture becomes a light caramel color. It'll be bubbling and oh so yummy-looking! It will reach pudding-like thickness. Remove pan from heat.

IT'S TIME TO ADD THE GOOD STUFF

- 1 cup coconut
- 1 cup pecans
- 1 tablespoon vanilla extract

BUILDING YOUR COOKIES

When the cookies are completely cooled, flip half of them over. Add a heaping tablespoon of the yummy frosting to each. Use the remaining cookies to top them off. Makes 10–12 sandwiches, depending on size.

Coconut Pecan Frosting

INGREDIENTS

- 2 cups pecans (chopped/diced)
- 1 can evaporated milk (12 ounces)
- 1½ cups sugar
- ¾ cup butter
- 6 egg yolks, lightly beaten
- 2 cups flaked coconut
- 1 teaspoon vanilla extract

You can toast your pecans in the oven if you like (at 350°F for about 7–10 minutes).

INSTRUCTIONS

Heat the evaporated milk, sugar, butter, and egg yolks in a heavy 3-qt. saucepan (medium heat). Don't stop stirring! Cook about 3 or 4 minutes. You'll know you're at the right point when the butter melts and the sugar is fully dissolved. Now, brace yourself! Time for a workout! Keep cooking (stirring nonstop) for 12–14 minutes or until mixture becomes a light caramel color. It'll be bubbling and oh so yummy looking! At this point it will reach a pudding-like thickness, which is perfection!

Remove pan from heat. It's time to add the coconut, vanilla, and pecans. Stir until they're incorporated. Now transfer the frosting to a bowl. It will take at least 30–45 minutes before it's ready to spread on the cake.

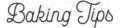

Baking Tips

TIE-DYEING WITH ROYAL ICING

This is a fun and colorful effect that's easy for people of all ages. Whether you're making T-shirt cookies, Christmas sweaters, or other themed cookies, tie-dying is the way to go.

WHAT YOU'LL NEED

- 1 bag royal icing, piping consistency
- 4–5 bags royal icing, flood consistency, in a variety of colors
- Baked cookies
- Toothpicks

HOW TO TIE-DYE

Start by outlining your cookie with the piping consistency icing to form a dam. Let it firm up about 10–15 minutes. Grab one bag of flood icing and apply it in a straight line, right to left. Directly under it, add a line in a different color. Keep going until you've used all the colors, then start over with the original color. Fill in the entire cookie. Now for the fun! Drag a toothpick from top to bottom down the center of the cookie. Repeat this process all the way across the cookie. If you want a "cabled" look (for Christmas sweaters, especially), drag the toothpick from bottom to top between the lines you've already added. The outcome is spectacular and looks like knitting!

Piping Designs on a Cake

If you've ever piped on a cake (buttercream- or fondant-covered), you know it can be a tricky process. Here are a few suggestions to make things easier.

- First, place the cake on a turntable for ease of movement. That way the cake can move and you won't have to.

- Second, have all of your piping bags prepped in advance and filled with icing.

- Third, speaking of icing: know which type works best for your project. For example, royal icing is the best for piping, but it can't be used on a buttercream cake or it will dissolve. Use royal for fondant-covered cakes and use buttercream or ganache for buttercream cakes.

- Fourth, if you have a particular design in mind, sketch it onto the cake with a toothpick. Don't make deep marks in case you need to change things up as you go.

- Fifth, the longer you hold onto that bag of piping icing, the warmer it will get in your hand. Always have a second bag handy when the first gets too mushy/soft.

- Finally, hold one hand to steady the other as you pipe. Your hand will get tired, so stop and rest as you are able.

There is little in life that could not benefit from a little love, a little time, and a stick of butter.

JULIA CHILD

Beat It!

INTRODUCTION

Life is hard. There's no predicting when difficult seasons will come—when a child will struggle in school, when a loved one will be diagnosed with illness, when a friend will abruptly walk away from a years-long friendship. You can't control these things, but you can get past them. We serve an overcoming God who has created us in His image. He doesn't want us to get stuck whenever a mountain rises in our path. Instead, He longs for us to speak to those mountains using words of faith and hope. In other words, He wants us to tap into His strength.

No matter what you're facing today, God can lift you out of it. Even the deepest depression or the darkest heartache can't help but fade when the Lord comes on the scene. It might seem impossible now, but better days are coming. And remember, God isn't asking you to be strong. He will be strong for you. He simply wants to remind you to put your faith and trust in Him.

What does all of this have to do with baking? Everything. Across this big, wide world, people are using baking as a form of therapy. It's an amazing way to step out from under the cloud of gloom and focus on something sweet. Plow through the issues in your heart as you work on that next cake project. Release your fears or anxieties as you roll out those sweet cookies. Let the mixing bowls pile up in the sink. Let the powdered sugar "poof" as it's mixed. Let the butter wrappers gather next to your work station. Who cares about the mess? It's worth it. Then, when all is said and done, look at that beautiful baked good and let it remind you that God wants to make something beautiful out of your mess, too. It will happen, you know. You will get through this. You are an overcomer.

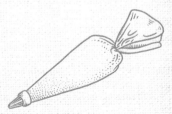

Loaves and Fishes...Transformed!

During the final weeks of my mother's life, I spent so many hours tending to her that I almost forgot about my youngest granddaughter's birthday. Jenna was turning four and I, the grandmother known for baking, had nothing for her. No cake. No cupcakes. No cookies. Nothing. To make matters even worse, Jenna was on her way to my house shortly to celebrate. I needed to get my act together...and quick!

I scoured the Internet and stumbled across a picture of a Beauty and the Beast cake. I could probably pull this off with a few common household items. But first, I had to make the cake.

I didn't have many ingredients on hand but finally settled on two common, kid-friendly flavors: chocolate and vanilla. I even managed to rustle up some fondant, which set my mind to reeling. I wouldn't have much time to decorate, but I wanted it to look as if I'd put in some effort.

After the cake finished baking, I covered the bottom tier in yellow fondant, cascading down to look like Belle's dress. I even added some red rosettes to dress it up. I covered the top tier in blue and designed it to look like the Beast's tuxedo, complete with white ruffle.

But what to do for the topper? This cake certainly didn't scream Beauty and the Beast. Not without the infamous rose.

I walked from room to room in my house, looking for ideas. When I clapped eyes on a large glass candle votive, I had my answer. I would flip it upside down and set it on top of the cake, putting a red rose inside.

As luck would have it, I had the perfect metal rose, red in color, to place inside what now appeared to look like a bell jar.

A short while later, my task was complete. Out of scraps and common household items, I'd pieced together a masterpiece. Jenna loved the cake. In fact, friends and family who saw the pictures proclaimed it to be one of my very best.

Isn't that what God manages to do with our lives? We give Him our not-yet-developed gifts, our limited abilities, our ordinariness, our flaws, our loaves and fishes. He breathes on those things, and...voilà! Something beautiful emerges. With His surge of heavenly power, we're transformed, in much the same way that the Beast morphed into a handsome prince. What a wonderful, gracious God we serve.

Do not conform to the pattern of this world,
but be transformed by the renewing of your mind.
Then you will be able to test
and approve what God's will is—
His good, pleasing and perfect will.
ROMANS 12:2 NIV

Prayer

Lord, even before the transformations in my life began, You saw the potential. You looked beyond my ordinariness and saw a masterpiece! I'm grateful for Your creative hand, Father, as You morph me into Your image. Amen.

A Midnight Run

It all started when I agreed to bake a three-tiered wedding cake for a friend's daughter. A simple task, really—no elaborate decor, just a frosted cake with a few silk flowers. I could've pulled off this one in my sleep. Funny how I almost had to.

I'd been working all afternoon, baking, filling, and frosting. Sometime around eleven that night, just as I wrapped up the stacking process, I realized that the cake wasn't standing up straight. *Strange*. All of the dowels were in place. The cakes were level. What went wrong?

I did my best to even out the layers but could tell the cake was unsteady. Something in the baking process must've gone awry because the bottom tier was simply...weak. While trying to shimmy the cake one last time, the whole thing gave way. Down she came, onto my kitchen table below.

Any other time I might've cried. Instead, I shoved the mess aside, grabbed my purse, and headed out to buy new ingredients. Now, I don't know about you, but shopping in the wee hours of the night has never been a favorite pastime of mine. Still, I had no choice. If I made it to the store in a hurry, I could get back home, bake nine layers (three tiers) of cake, whip up more frosting, stack, and decorate. Would I get any sleep? Probably not, but what did it matter at this point? A bride would be waiting at 11:00 a.m. and I would not disappoint her.

So, off to the store I went. An hour later I was back home in a baking frenzy. About five hours after that, I tucked the three-tiered beauty (blissfully secure) into the fridge to chill while I caught a couple of hours' sleep.

This incident reminded me of many times God has come racing out into dark places to give me a second chance, a fresh start. He's navigated dark and winding roads to teach and reteach lessons. I can almost picture Him now, pushing the broken layers of my life aside, just as I pushed those broken cake layers onto my kitchen table. He's always ready to begin a new work.

Aren't you grateful the Lord offers do-overs? Aren't you glad He didn't give up on you when you needed to begin again? What a gracious and forgiving God we serve!

You have searched me, LORD, and You know me. You know when I sit and when I rise; You perceive my thoughts from afar. You discern my going out and my lying down; You are familiar with all my ways.

PSALM 139:1–3 NIV

Prayer

Lord, thank You for traversing the darkness of night to track me down and help me begin again. I don't always get it right the first time (or second or third, now that I think about it) but You are always willing to offer a do-over. How I love and appreciate You, my gracious Father! Amen.

Trading Spaces

After my mother passed away, I moved from our spacious home into a small town house. Talk about an abrupt change! My new space was lovely but tiny. I'd traded in a massive kitchen island for a small one. This, of course, cramped my style. Many times over, I found myself pining for my old kitchen with its endless counter space.

Figuring out how to organize in a small space is hard enough, but when you're baking a cake, it's near to impossible. I found this out the hard way when I arrived home from the grocery store and couldn't even find adequate space to put the bags down. How could I ever manage in such tight quarters? I just kept bumping into things. And worse yet, I could never find the items I needed. Some were outside in the storage closet. Others were in the coat closet at the foot of the stairs. Ugh. About six months into my move I started having buyer's remorse. How could I be grateful for the situation I now found myself in?

Over time I've learned to adjust to my new kitchen. I've had new countertops installed and have enlarged the island. I've gotten creative with my storage abilities. I've got things tucked away in all kinds of random places. It works for me. I've decorated my kitchen in a quaint farmhouse style that suits my personality.

What about you? What is your kitchen space like? What sort of kitchen do you dream of? If you take the time to organize and plan, you can turn your current space into the best it can be. Instead of bemoaning all that you don't have, let God show you what He can do with a little creative thinking. Most of all, learn to be grateful for what you have. You might not live in a mansion or have a dream kitchen, but you are right where God placed you, and He will give you all you need to get the job done.

Every good gift
and every perfect gift is from above,
coming down from the Father of lights
with whom there is no variation
or shadow due to change.
JAMES 1:17 ESV

Prayer

Lord, I don't want to be a grumbler. I'm so grateful for my home and my kitchen. I'm counting on You to give me creative ideas. I want to organize and decorate so that this space is fully usable. Thanks for Your help, Father. Amen.

Four Daughters, Four Weddings, Four Years

It was inevitable, I suppose. When you have four daughters, you know the weddings will eventually come. I just didn't expect them to all come within four years of each other.

My oldest got married in 2004 on Valentine's weekend. We hosted a beautiful Italian-themed event, with shades of deep red and gold. Back in those days, I wasn't baking yet, so we hired someone to make the cake. I had sticker shock when they quoted me the price, but what could I do? I paid for the cake, of course. Unfortunately, about two-thirds of the cake came home with us after the reception.

Four and a half months later, my second daughter got married. She had this crazy idea that I could bake her wedding cake to save money. I'd never done anything like that at the time but tried a practice run for her shower, and the little tiered cake turned out okay. On the day of the wedding a couple of friends with decorating experience showed up to help me. Between us, we created a wedding cake even lovelier than the one for daughter number one.

Then came daughter number three. Tragedy struck our family on the week of her wedding. My forty-five-year-old sister passed away unexpectedly in her sleep three days before the wedding. I was in no shape to bake but had no choice. I stayed up all night making the cakes and then passed the individual tiers off to a baking buddy, who constructed the Hawaiian-themed cake for me. It was tropical and lovely.

By the time we got to daughter number four, I felt like an old pro. Her cake was a simple design and I managed it by myself. Over the four years, though, I learned a lot.

What about you? Are you on a learning curve? What area of your life requires the most growth right now? Do you plan to move forward, to learn the lessons that need to be learned? If you do, beautiful things await you on the opposite end of your journey.

Let the wise hear
and increase in learning,
and the one who understands
obtain guidance.
PROVERBS 1:5 ESV

Prayer

Lord, I want to be a perpetual learner. May I be Your ready student, growing and developing in the gifts You've given me. You're such a gentle teacher, Father, and I'm grateful to be on a learning curve with You as my guide. Amen.

Stabilized Whipped Cream

One of my favorite cakes is strawberry lemonade. It's light, refreshing, and hits all the right notes. I love making this cake in the spring and summer because it fits the mood of most casual parties. And I have yet to find a person who doesn't love it. Those berries really hit the spot.

It starts with a luscious lemon cake, light and fluffy. Between the layers I add lemon curd, strawberry preserves, and/or slices of fresh strawberries, along with stabilized whipped cream.

What's stabilized whipped cream, you ask? It's a heavier-than-usual variety of the whipped cream you've grown to love, one that can withstand the weight of the layers without breaking down into mush when the damp strawberries are added. This is critical because you don't want a wet cake.

After the various layers are stacked, I fill a piping bag with some of the whipped cream and pipe it onto the top of the cake in little puffs. Then I decorate with fresh strawberries. (The sides of this cake are left bare, which gives it a bit of that naked cake feel, perfect for a spring or summer event.)

If I'm being honest, I would have to say that my life journey has reminded me a lot of that stabilized whipped cream. Without the stability of the Lord, I'm a mushy mess. Every little thing that comes along causes me to break down. Sure, I try to hold up on my own, but without His support, I'll fail every time. My proverbial cake will crumble.

What about you? Have you ever tried to go it alone without God's support or wisdom? Did your efforts fail or succeed? How did you find your way back to Him?

God longs for us to grow and develop in Him, and that means sticking close. Sure, He wants us to step out in faith and try new things, but only under the umbrella of His covering. So keep Him front and center in your life and your cake will stand straight and tall.

He drew me up
from the pit of destruction,
out of the miry bog,
and set my feet upon a rock,
making my steps secure.
PSALM 40:2 ESV

Prayer

Lord, on my own I'm not very stable. Sure, I think I'm tough. I'm sure I can handle anything that comes my way. But without You, I crumble. Thank You for the reminder that my stability should remain in You. I'll stick close, Lord. Amen.

Dueling Gender-Reveal Cakes

Have you ever tried to bake with a house full of company, especially little ones? I found myself in that predicament while baking a gender-reveal cake for a customer who was having a little boy. Only, she didn't know she was having a little boy. I received a call from her OB/GYN's office. The nurse clued me in so that I would know to make the inside of the cake blue.

No problem! I mixed up the batter, layered the cake, and went to work swirling pink buttercream rosettes on one side of the cake and blue rosettes on the other. Which side would the mom- and dad-to-be choose? Would they be tickled blue when they cut into the cake to discover that they were having a boy?

In the middle of baking this cake, one of my houseguests informed me that she had a friend who needed a gender-reveal cake, too. That same day, in fact. We gathered the necessary information, and before long I was baking a second gender-reveal cake, this one pink on the inside. I decorated the outside exactly the same—pink rosettes on one side, blue on the other.

Only one problem. Now both gender-reveal cakes sat side by side on the table, and they looked exactly alike. If not for the fact that one was slightly larger than the other, I might have given the wrong cake to the wrong family! Oops!

I got to thinking about how decision-making is a lot like that. We look at two different choices and they both look equally good to us. Should we take this job or that job? Should we move to this neighborhood or that neighborhood? Decisions, decisions, decisions!

Aren't you glad that God knows what is best for us? And if we're listening, He's whispering, "Take this one, not that one." Whew! Where would we be without His guidance?

> *Trust in the LORD with all your heart,*
> *and do not lean on your own understanding.*
> *In all your ways acknowledge him,*
> *and he will make straight your paths.*
> PROVERBS 3:5–6 ESV

Lord, I'm so grateful You're right there to guide me. Otherwise I'd be so confused. I'd look at all of the prospects in front of me and not know which road to take. I love Your gentle whispers: "Turn to the right" or "Turn to the left." They come at just the right time. I appreciate Your kindness, Lord. Amen.

Better Together

I love a good cookies-and-cream cake. There's something about the merging of chocolate and vanilla that gets me every time, and the crunch from the crumbled cookies gives it that extra *wow* factor. This tasty treat is a favorite with my grandkids, too.

I came up with my own strategy for this cake a few years back but had to test it out to make sure it would work. I wanted the cake to look like a real sandwich cookie when you cut into it, so I baked three ten-inch layers—two chocolate and one white. I sandwiched the white between the chocolate. In between those layers I added a thick helping of buttercream, which I'd loaded with chopped-up Oreos. Talk about delectable! When I finished the stacking process, I covered the whole cake in the cookies-and-cream frosting and then placed Oreos around the bottom of the cake. I finished it off with a cookie on top.

Now, I don't know about you, but there's something about cookies-and-cream that's hard to resist. When I cut into the cake, it really looked like a giant cookie. Not that I got to look at it for long. Everyone in the house wanted to dive right in.

I got to thinking about that cake, about how the colors looked so beautiful, merged together like that. My heart grew sad as I thought about how racially divided many people around me had become. I wanted to slice up a giant piece of cookies-and-cream cake to serve everyone. If they could taste and see how sweet those two flavors were, sitting side by side, surely they would understand that loving others—even those vastly different from themselves—was equally as sweet.

We have a long way to go before racial division ends, but it can start today in your heart. Love others as Christ loves you. The transformation in your heart will be sweet in His eyes and offer love and hope to all you come in contact with.

> *A new commandment I give to you,*
> *that you love one another:*
> *just as I have loved you,*
> *you also are to love one another.*
> JOHN 13:34 ESV

Prayer

Father, may I never forget that we are better together. May the color of our skin never divide us. May we stand fast together, a sweet reminder that You created us all to love and be loved in return. Amen.

Waller Out a Hole

My friend Crystal is a hoot. She's a country girl through and through—more at home canning squirrel meat than shopping at a high-end grocery store. Her rich Texas twang captivates me and makes every story more fun to listen to. And, boy, does she have stories!

Crystal also happens to be an amazing baker. She often shows up at events with homemade breads, croissants, and so on. Even better than her breads are her baking stories. She recently shared one that had me laughing so hard, I could barely breathe. It involved her grandma Dixon's homemade drop biscuits.

It all started when she attempted to explain how to add the wet ingredients to the dry. "Just waller out a hole," she said.

Now, I'm a baker. I know the phraseology. But this "waller out a hole" phrase, I'd never heard before.

"What does that mean?" I asked.

Crystal looked at me, clearly puzzled at my lack of knowledge. She gestured with her hands, moving them in a circular motion. "You know...waller out a hole."

"Um, nope. Never heard that one before."

The stares from Crystal continued. "You know," she said, "you push the flour to the sides and waller out a hole in the middle of it to put the eggs."

"Ohh." I got it. Wallering out a hole meant making room for more ingredients.

I've thought about that expression a lot since then. Sometimes I'm so busy, so distracted, that I don't waller out a hole for God. I don't make room for Him in my daily life. I try to sprinkle Him in like baking soda instead of deliberately making room for the good stuff.

What about you? Have you wallered out a hole for God today? Better push the busywork aside and make room for Him. And while you're at it, waller out a hole for your friends and family, too. When you do that, everything comes out just fine.

Draw near to God,
and he will draw near to you.
Cleanse your hands, you sinners,
and purify your hearts,
you double-minded.
JAMES 4:8 ESV

Prayer

Father, I don't ever want to be so busy that I leave You out. You're the reason I exist, the reason I put one foot in front of the other each day. I'll make room for You, Lord, and for those I love, as well. Thank You for the reminder. Amen.

Marching One by One

I arrived home late one night to discover that an army of ants had invaded my kitchen. This is never good for any homeowner, but it's particularly tough for a baker!

The little critters had marched in a single-file line from the back door to the dog food bowl, which was on the far side of the room. I'd never seen so many ants in one place in my life and certainly not in such an orderly fashion. It was as if they had a plan to take over my life. They wanted me to know they were serious.

Of course, I went to work at trying to kill them all, but they refused to die. Day in and day out I battled them, often growing angry and fearful as they continued their rampage. Those pesky critters turned up in my cabinets, on my floor, and even in my sugar container. Ugh!

Only when I dealt with the little fellows aggressively did they finally take their leave...and good riddance. May I never see another ant in my house again!

As I pondered those little devils, I got to thinking about the little nuisances in my life, the things I've allowed in that should not be there—gossip, overeating, overspending, and so on. These "little foxes" (as the Bible calls them) might seem like minuscule things, and by themselves they aren't very troublesome. But when you line them up, one by one, they can do a lot of damage. They can infiltrate the whole of your life and wreak havoc.

What about you? What "ants" have you allowed into your life? It's time to deal aggressively with them, to call them what they are...enemies. To get rid of an enemy, you have to look him in the eye and tell him to get lost. Exterminate him! Shoo him out the door, never to return. Only then will you live in a place of safety and peace.

> Catch the foxes for us,
> the little foxes that spoil the vineyards,
> for our vineyards are in blossom.
> SONG OF SOLOMON 2:15 ESV

Prayer

Lord, I let so many irritations get in my way. Instead of dealing with them on the spot, I allow them to build up until they seem like ants invading my territory. Show me how to deal with them one by one, I pray. I'll be so glad to see them gone! Amen.

Ahoy, Matey!

When I'm not busy in the kitchen, I direct plays at a local Christian theater. I always have a blast working with the incoming cast members. Over the years I've set a precedent of baking for them. It usually starts a few weeks into rehearsals with something simple, like cookies. Then, as we get closer to the show, my treats increase in intensity. This makes no sense, because I'm already drowning in work at the theater. But a baker's gotta bake. And I love my kiddos, so creating sweet treats for them is pure joy.

A couple of years back we did a pirate-themed play. I decided to bake some round sugar cookies and paint them to look like pirate faces. I had the best time putting them together. They were colorful and fun. But as we drew near to the cast party on the final day, I knew I had to offer something extraordinary, so I decided to bake and decorate a cake to look like a real pirate ship.

Now, I'd done a couple of the pirate-ship cakes before, but not for such a large crowd. This thing needed to be large enough to feed fifty people. I started with a sheet cake on the bottom. I frosted it in blue and swirled the icing to look like water. There! I had my ocean. Then I began the tedious process of cutting, stacking, and maneuvering layers until they were shaped like a ship. Finally content, I added a layer of frosting and then covered the whole thing in fondant. After several decorative bits, I'd created a realistic-looking ship. This process was tedious and grueling, but I wanted to do my best for those I loved.

Maybe you can relate. Perhaps there are those in your life who require extra effort. You're already tired. You don't know if you have it in you to go the extra mile. But you know in your gut it's the right thing to do. So you persevere. You don't give up. You keep on working until the task is complete, because the one you love is worth it.

Let us not become weary in doing good,
for at the proper time we will reap a harvest
if we do not give up.
GALATIANS 6:9 NIV

Prayer

I won't give up, Lord. You've given me tasks to perform and people to care for, and they are worth every bit of effort. May I never forget that my service to them is a reflection of Your love for me. I want to love as You love, Father, and serve as You serve. Help me, I pray. Amen.

Dump Cake

My son-in-law, Kevin, loves to make dessert at impromptu family gatherings. Because these get-togethers are usually unplanned, we don't always have all the ingredients necessary for a full-out dessert. So he makes his infamous dump cake.

Now, I don't know about you, but I like it when things are simple, and nothing's simpler than a dump cake. Kevin takes a can of fruit (usually peaches) and dumps it into a baking dish. Then he spreads dry cake mix on top. He takes a stick of butter, slices it, and places the slices all over the cake mix. (He's rather meticulous about this process, which is a lot of fun to watch. I'm not the only one in the family with a baking gene.)

He pops the concoction into the oven and bakes it until it's golden. Then it's time to eat. Wow, what an amazingly simple sweet treat, one everyone enjoys. Best of all, you can change up the fruit so that it's different each time. Apples. Cherries. Blueberries. You name it, dump cake is the perfect medium for it.

Sometimes simple is best, especially if you're with family. Because you're comfortable around one another, you're not out to impress. There's no audience, just those you love. You can relax and be yourself. Who cares if the dump cake is a little gooey or if bits of the cake mix didn't quite get incorporated into the juice of the fruit? The point of the cake is its simplicity, its ease. After all, being with family trumps baking any day.

So the next time you need a quick and easy dish, look no further than your pantry for canned fruit and a cake mix in the flavor of your choice. Before long you'll settle into a comfortable spot at the table. (And by the way, dump cake is perfect with a big scoop of vanilla ice cream on top!)

Our boast is this,
the testimony of our conscience,
that we behaved in the world
with simplicity and godly sincerity,
not by earthly wisdom but by the grace of God,
and supremely so toward you.
II CORINTHIANS 1:12 ESV

Father, I love it when I can keep things simple. Too often I strive to impress, but when I'm with my family, I can settle in and enjoy our time together without putting on a show. Thank You for teaching me that I'm accepted and loved. Amen.

An Ever-Present Help

Our family's annual Easter egg hunt happened to take place on the same day I was scheduled to deliver a four-tiered wedding cake to a venue on the opposite side of town. No problem. I had my day timed down to the minute.

My daughter happened to be coordinating the wedding, so she left our family gathering ahead of me to make her way north to the wedding party. I stayed behind visiting with family, knowing I would have to leave when the clock struck three o'clock. At exactly 2:57 my granddaughter, who was in my care, did a flip on the trampoline and hit her head on the metal railing. I've never seen so much blood in my life.

With no other course of action making sense, I raced her to urgent care. They felt her wound would require more care, so we were asked to transfer her to the hospital. My other daughter (who happened to be with me, also caring for this grandchild) had to take it from there. I had a cake to pick up from home, deliver to a wedding venue, put together, and decorate.

The next hour and a half was a blur. I somehow made it to my house, grabbed the four individual cakes, loaded them into my car, and headed north to the venue (which was about fifty-five minutes away). When I got there, the wedding party was lined up, ready to walk down the aisle. I went to work, stacking and decorating. Talk about stressed!

The cake turned out fine. In fact, the venue and the cake both had a very rustic feel, so there was no need for perfection. The minute I wrapped up the decorating, I got back into my car and drove south for over an hour until I reached the hospital, just as my granddaughter was getting stitches.

Sometimes life is like that. Things get complicated. They pile up. You have tough decisions to make in the moment. Trust the Holy Spirit to guide you every minute of the way. He is our ever-present help in time of trouble, after all!

> *Cast your burden on the LORD,*
> *and he will sustain you;*
> *he will never permit the righteous*
> *to be moved.*
> PSALM 55:22 ESV

Prayer

Lord, I'm so glad I can depend on You when the going gets rough. You haven't fallen off Your throne. You're still right there, leading, guiding, speaking. I'm grateful for Your ever-present help in my times of trouble, Father. Amen.

The Four Seasons

Cookie-decorating classes are a blast, but they are so much work! The day before the event I have to bake hundreds of cookies, usually four per participant. Then I have to prepare enough royal icing to fill forty-eight to sixty piping bags, all in various colors, of course.

My friend Carolyn asked me to teach a Bible study at her church and incorporate a cookie-decorating class. No problem. I decided to speak on Nehemiah. The gist of my message was that Nehemiah, like all of us, went through various seasons in his walk with God: winter, when he was in mourning over the wall that had broken down; spring, when his hopes began to rise as a new plan to build motivated him; summer, as the work was in full force; and autumn, as the work came to an end.

For the cookie-decorating part, I made season-themed cookies, enough that each lady could have all four seasons represented. For summer I made surfboard cookies. For fall I baked cookies that looked like leaves. For winter, gorgeous snowflakes, and for spring I did beautiful flowers. I taught my lesson and then we turned our attention to the cookies. Those ladies had a blast, and so did I. All my work was rewarded as I watched them with piping bags in hand.

Isn't that just how life is? We work so hard in some seasons. Then things slow down a bit (and we're grateful). God designed the (literal) seasons as a reminder that tough times (winter seasons) won't last forever. They will burst forth into spring. And just like those beautiful flower-themed cookies, our hearts will come alive again.

What season are you in right now? Are new ideas bursting forth in a springtime season? Are you in full-out work mode, in the middle of your summer? Do things seem to be winding down in your autumn? Are you wondering if the frost will ever lift in your winter?

No matter where you are, God is right there with you, and He wants you to know that another season is just around the bend.

> *There is a time for everything,*
> *and a season for every activity*
> *under the heavens.*
> ECCLESIASTES 3:1 NIV

Prayer

Father, I'm so grateful that seasons don't last forever. I've been through some tough winters, when I thought the ice and snow would never melt. But You performed a miracle! You turned things around and gave me a lovely spring. May I never doubt Your seasons, Lord!

Strawberry-Lemonade Cake

INGREDIENTS

CAKE
- 1 boxed cake mix, white
- 1 boxed cake mix, lemon
- 1 cup water
- 2 tablespoons lemon juice
- ¼ cup oil
- 6 egg whites

FILLING
- Lemon curd
- 2 pints of fresh strawberries, sliced
- ¼ cup powdered sugar

FROSTING
- 1 large container heavy whipping cream
- ¼ cup sugar
- 1 package instant lemon pudding

INSTRUCTIONS

Start by whipping the egg whites for about a minute. Slowly and carefully incorporate other cake ingredients. When batter is thoroughly mixed, divide it into three 10-inch pans. (It will make thin layers, which is what you want.) Bake at 350°F until cakes spring to the touch. Don't overcook. The thinner layers will take a bit less time than the usual 30 minutes, depending on your oven.

Prepare the filling by pouring the entire container of lemon curd into a bowl and stirring until smooth.

Now it's time to prepare the fruit. Wash and slice 2 pints fresh strawberries. Sprinkle with ¼ cup powdered sugar and place in refrigerator.

In a separate bowl, make stabilized whipped cream: Whip cream to soft peaks. Add ¼ cup sugar and 1 box instant lemon pudding. Whip until the mixture reaches a creamy consistency.

Time to stack! Start with the first layer of cake. Spread the top of it with lemon curd, then pipe a dam around the edges using the whipped cream. Add the berries, avoiding as much of the juice as possible and leaving the dam intact.

Top it off with the lemon-flavored whipped cream (which you can pipe on in spiral fashion). Then add the next cake, top it with lemon curd, add berries, whipped cream, and so on, until you reach the top. Frost with whipped cream and add extra dollops of whipped cream with berries on top for decoration. There's no need to frost the sides of the cake. Instead, press some strawberry slices into the gaps between the layers.

Variations on Stabilized Whipped Cream

INGREDIENTS

- 1 large container heavy whipping cream
- ¼ cup sugar
- 1 package instant pudding (in any flavor you like)

Whip the cream to soft peaks. Add ¼ cup sugar. Add full box of instant pudding. Mix until the whipped cream takes on a creamy consistency.

For additional choices, choose from the following pudding flavors:

- Lemon
- Vanilla
- Chocolate
- Butterscotch
- Banana cream
- White chocolate

These stabilized whipped creams are luscious when used with fruits.

Cookie Butter Cake

CAKE INGREDIENTS

- 1 white cake mix
- ¼ cup crushed Lotus Biscoff cookies
- 1 teaspoon cinnamon
- ½ teaspoon pumpkin pie spice
- ½ cup oil
- ½ cup melted cookie butter
- 2 tablespoons brown sugar (or 1 tablespoon maple syrup/pancake syrup)
- 3 eggs
- 1¼ cups milk
- Additional crushed Lotus Biscoff cookies (to top off before baking)

FROSTING INGREDIENTS

- 1 block cream cheese
- 1½ cups softened butter
- ⅓ cup cookie butter
- 1 tablespoon maple syrup
- 1 teaspoon cinnamon
- ¼ teaspoon pumpkin pie spice
- 5–6 cups powdered sugar
- 1 teaspoon vanilla

Cookie Butter Cake
(CONTINUED)

INSTRUCTIONS

Combine cake mix, crushed cookies, and spices and mix thoroughly. Add oil, melted cookie butter, and brown sugar or maple syrup and mix until crumbly. Add eggs, one at a time.

Gradually add milk and mix until smooth. Spoon batter into cupcake liners and sprinkle approximately 1 tablespoon crushed Biscoff cookies on top; then bake at 350°F for 15 minutes (or until done). When cupcakes are cooled, top with frosting and finish off with melted cookie butter and cookie crumbs. Press half a cookie into each cupcake.

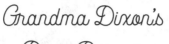

Grandma Dixon's Drop Biscuits

THE COUNTRY WAY

INGREDIENTS

- 6 heaping dinner tablespoons of flour
- 1½ teaspoons of baking powder
- A sprinkling of sugar
- A dash of salt
- A dollop of buttermilk
- 1 tablespoon butter

INSTRUCTIONS

Combine dry ingredients. Waller out a hole in the middle. Place butter in the hole and add the milk. Stir to form dough (it will be sticky). Drop spoonfuls of dough into greased biscuit or muffin pan *or* drop spoonfuls of dough in flour bin, coat ball, dust off extra, and place in greased medium-size cast-iron skillet. Repeat until pan is full. Should make six biscuits. Bake in preheated 400°F oven until golden.

Grandma Dixon's
Drop Biscuits

THE MEASURED WAY

INGREDIENTS

- 1 cup flour
- ½ teaspoon salt
- ½ teaspoon sugar
- 2 teaspoons baking powder
- 1 tablespoon buttermilk
- 1 tablespoon butter

INSTRUCTIONS

Combine dry ingredients. Waller out a hole in the middle. Place butter in the hole and add the milk. Stir to form dough (will be sticky). Drop spoonfuls of dough into greased biscuit or muffin pan *or* drop spoonfuls of dough in flour bin, coat ball, dust off extra, and place in greased medium-size cast-iron skillet. Repeat until pan is full. Should make six biscuits. Bake in preheated 400°F oven until golden.

Tips

THE ZEBRA TECHNIQUE

If you're looking for a way to wow your guests, this will do the trick. Create a cake in two or even three or more colors. This isn't your grandma's marble cake, though. With a simple strategy, you can create a cake that slices to look exactly like zebra stripes on the inside.

For the sake of explanation, I'll use two colors, white and brown (chocolate). Mix your batters and prep your baking pans. Start with one scoop (about half a cup) of white batter in the bottom/center of your pan. Then add a scoop of chocolate batter, directly on top. The pressure from the chocolate batter will cause the white cake batter to spread a bit, forming a ring around the outside.

Continue adding alternating batters until the pan is about half full. Then tap the pan against the countertop to remove any bubbles and allow the colors to merge. When you look down into the pan you'll see rings (like tree rings). Don't worry! They might not look like a zebra now, but once you build two or three layers of cake, the effect will spring to life as you cut into it.

This is also fun to do with rainbow colors. To offset the vivid colors, add a scoop of white between every colorful layer.

NOTE: When I do a gender-reveal cake, I'll often bake the inside in zebra fashion—blue and white for a boy and pink and white for a girl.

Organizational Tips

If you love to bake but you're having trouble keeping all the "stuff" organized, here are a few tips to help you out.

STORAGE/COOKIE CUTTERS

Cookies cutters are fun to collect but they're a pain to store. Start by dividing your cookie cutters by theme. Seasonal cutters in one bin/basket, Valentine's in another, summer cookies in another, Christmas in another, and so on. Smaller collections (sports-themed cutters, animals, etc.) can be put into gallon-sized baggies and placed into bins. On the outside of each bin, write what's inside so that you can tell at a glance which bin to grab.

STORAGE/CAKE PANS

Cake pans are huge and take up a lot of space. I purchased a large baker's rack (the tallest I could find at the home improvement store) and placed it in a storage closet. I divided the shelves by types of pans. I did my best to stack "like" pans together: 6", 8", 10", 12", and 14" are stored together, and 5", 7", and 9" are stored together. All square pans have their own spot, as do the rectangular. I also created a shelf for extraneous stuff like cake domes, cake boards, oversized rolling pins, and so on. There's also a spot for turntables and large decorative items. Smaller items like fondant molds are kept together as well. I know at a glance which items are where.

BE PREPARED

Before you start baking that cake or cookies, make sure you have everything you need nearby. Ingredients, rolling pins, parchment paper, floured baking spray, waxed paper to roll sugar cookies on... whatever you need, have it close by. This is especially true of things like cooling racks. They should be out on the table and ready before any of those pans go into the oven. Empty your dishwasher before you start because you'll need someplace to put all those dirty dishes. There's nothing worse than getting halfway into a project and running out of counter space because there's nowhere to put the batter-covered mixing bowls.

WORKSPACE TIP

Use a bench scraper to clear your workspace of crumbs and leftover bits of this and that.

OVEN TIPS

If your oven bakes unevenly, no problem. Just rotate the pans inside every ten minutes. If I have two pans on the top rack and two on the bottom, I rotate them counterclockwise, one at a time, so that all of the cakes have an opportunity to bake evenly.

TAKE CARE OF YOU

Drink water...and lots of it. Most bakers get wrapped up in their projects and forget to drink. I've had many a migraine as a result of dehydration. Prep the glass or water bottle in advance and have it handy. Remember to sit down on occasion and rest those weary feet. They need a break! Listen to your favorite music while you bake. Sing to your heart's content.

Count the memories, not the calories.

ANONYMOUS

The Sweet Life

INTRODUCTION

Think back over your life. How many of your favorite memories took place in someone's kitchen? If you're like most, you can probably remember all sorts of wonderful kitchen-based adventures.

Maybe you have childhood memories of being in your grandparents' home, watching grandma bake her delicious homemade bread. Or perhaps you spent a few days at your cousin's place, where your aunt taught you to roll out pie crust. Maybe your mother showed you how to paint sugar cookies at Christmastime or decorate a cake with sprinkles. Perhaps an elderly neighbor blessed you with her mint chocolate chip cookie recipe. These precious memories linger because each one involved a loved one pouring into your life and passing on new skills.

Now it's your turn! You get to pass on what you learned to the next generation. You can swing wide your doors and encourage others to make new, fresh memories that will affect the generation after them.

And why not? So many of life's stories begin in the kitchen, after all. In that precious place, children can learn math, science, and culinary skills. They also learn to observe while mom (or dad) uses God-given creative skills. More than anything, they are included. They are wanted. They are loved...in the kitchen.

And that feeling of being wanted carries over into their adult life, where they duplicate the message by sharing it with their children, grandchildren, nieces, nephews, and friends.

What memories have you made in your kitchen of late? If you can't think of any, maybe it's time to start. God designed you for fellowship, after all, and what better place to congregate than the kitchen? So gather those bowls! Reach for the ingredients. Then make that call to a friend or loved one, so that you're not alone when those culinary confections are created. There are plenty of joys to be had when you bake together.

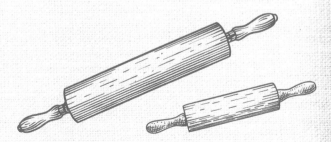

Mama's Country Kitchen

For years, my mama lived in a house in the country. She and my stepdad had sixty-three acres, complete with horses, cows, goats, and chickens. The place just screamed, "Come and visit!"

One of my favorite things about taking my kiddos up to see their grandparents was Mama's kitchen. She'd decorated it in shades of country blue, perfect for the location. But what really wowed me were the things she created in that amazing place. Mama always cooked a big lunch, usually around eleven in the morning. Evening hours were spent snacking on popcorn, ice cream, or peaches. She lived near a peach orchard, so her freezer was always filled with bags of ripe, delicious peaches. And the pecan tree in the backyard ensured bags of shelled pecans in the freezer, too.

Mama knew how to take the things she had on hand—meat from her own stock, vegetables from her garden, peaches from the orchard, and pecans from the backyard tree—to make the most amazing meals. And, boy, could she make some delectable desserts. Snickerdoodles, glazed sugar cookies, Texas sheet cake, Ranger cookies, fudge...you could always count on something special from Mama's kitchen.

Since my mother passed away, the mantle has fallen to me. Now I'm the grandmother ushering the little ones into her kitchen. And do they love it at my place! They know that when they come to Nina's house there will always be sweet treats and lots of love. The mixer is usually prepped and ready and the rolling pins are out. The cake pans are greased and floured and the bags of powdered sugar are on the counter, in preparation. These sweet traditions are the things memories are made of, after all.

In the same way that Mama would woo us to her kitchen with fresh, homemade treats, the Lord bids us to come into His presence. There's a sweetness there you won't find elsewhere. He doesn't look at you and say, "You messed up today. You're not welcome." Instead, no matter what you've done, He's standing with arms wide open, ready to welcome you home.

> *Where shall I go from your Spirit?*
> *Or where shall I flee from your presence?*
> PSALM 139:7 ESV

Prayer

I love the sweet memories of my mom's kitchen, Lord. I always felt so comfortable, so welcome there. You make me feel the same way, Father! No matter what I'm going through in this life, I know that I'm always at home with You. Amen.

Open Heart, Open Kitchen, Open Life

When I need to tackle a big baking job (say, hundreds of Valentine's cookies or a four-tiered wedding cake), I call on a couple of people to help me. My friend April is terrific in the kitchen. She's a hard worker and has a sweet personality. Then there's my daughter Megan. She's hysterical. She keeps us laughing for hours on end.

One night, April and Megan came over to help me bake, along with a couple of other friends. Talk about a full house! We asked my Amazon Alexa to play some of our favorite oldies songs. Boy, did we have fun! We got so tickled when each song played, because it brought back such memories from years gone by. Before long, we were all singing at the top of our lungs while we baked, baked, baked the night away. In between the songs we would swap stories, share memories, and basically crack each other up.

There's no better way to pass the time when you have a big project than to laugh with those you love. Gathered there, around my big kitchen island, it felt more like a party than a task to be performed. Somewhere between the songs, the laughter, and the sweet conversation, I almost forgot I was working at all.

Isn't that just how life should be? Instead of focusing on the size of the task, maybe it's time to focus on the joy in the journey. When you're surrounded by encouragers and helpers, even the most overwhelming task can seem doable. No man is an island, after all. If you've been hiding yourself away, it's time to get brave and step out. If you're feeling like you don't have a team of helpers, then offer to help someone else. When you give of yourself in this way, you bring joy not only to others but to yourself as well. It's time to adopt a new motto: open heart, open kitchen, open life.

He will yet fill your mouth with laughter,
and your lips with shouting.
JOB 8:21 ESV

Prayer

Lord, I don't ever want to do life alone. Surround me with the people You long to see in my life, Lord...people who can encourage, uplift, and draw me closer to You. And please point me in the direction of people who need my encouragement as well. Amen.

Life Is Short: Lick the Bowl

In order to become an official bakery business, I had to take a couple of state-mandated courses online and then test afterward. No worries. I sailed right through all that. Most of the material had to do with cleanliness, hygiene, food temperatures, and so on.

I've been very careful to follow regulations. It's not always easy when the grandkids come over, especially when they want to help. That doesn't happen much when I'm baking for customers, though.

I really ran into a problem when my mother's Alzheimer's progressed. Keeping her hands clean (especially during those final months) was tough, so I made sure she was preoccupied in front of a TV show while I worked, to keep her from sticking her fingers in the bowls (something she loved to do).

One day I worked for hours and hours on a cake. I whipped up a ton of buttercream and frosted the cake, then set it in the fridge to chill. I'd left a small amount of frosting in the bowl on the kitchen counter, which I planned to put into a piping bag and save.

When I came back into the kitchen I found my mother deliriously happy, fingers in the bowl. She licked them, flashed a big smile, and then stuck her hand in again.

I got a sinking feeling in my gut right away. There went my buttercream. Just as quickly, I caught another glimpse of the look of pure delight on my mother's face. In that moment, I realized the truth: I would rather lose an entire batch of buttercream... start over, even...than to wipe that smile off my mom's face. It was worth it. She was worth it.

My mom passed away about a month after that event. So many memories have flitted through my mind since her passing, but the buttercream incident remains in the forefront. I'd make a hundred batches more if I could only see that mischievous smile.

Maybe you can relate. Maybe you've lost a loved one, too. Maybe you'd give anything to have one more moment (even an inconvenient one) just to have that person back. I understand. God does, too. He gives us precious memories so that we never, ever forget those we love. Why not spend a few minutes thanking Him for those memories, even now?

I know that there is nothing better for people than to be happy and to do good while they live. That each of them may eat and drink, and find satisfaction in all their toil—this is the gift of God.
ECCLESIASTES 3:12–13 NIV

Prayer

Lord, I'm so grateful for the wonderful mentors You've placed in my life. I'm happy for the reminder that some things are far more important than a silly bowl of frosting. Buttercream may come and go, but the joy of seeing a smile on a loved one's face will last forever. I praise You for these amazing people, Father. Amen.

Peyton's Baking Party

My granddaughter Peyton informed me that she wanted to have a baking party on her tenth birthday. She asked if I would host the event at my house, since I had the necessary tools (and space). I joyfully agreed. I did a lot of baking in advance. I made enough T-shirt–shaped cookies for each of the girls to "tie-dye" with icing. And I baked several tiny (three-layer, six-inch) cakes for the girls to decorate.

On the day of the party, we set up the table with all sorts of sweet baking-themed decor. At each place setting we set a chef's hat and apron. The first order of business when the eight girls arrived was to let them decorate their aprons and hats. Once that business was behind us, they donned their new attire and we got busy baking cupcakes. The girls did the measuring, mixing, and scooping, and I managed the running of the oven.

While the cupcakes baked, the girls got busy decorating their tie-dyed cookies with royal icing. I marveled at how realistic they looked. Then the party guests turned their attention to their individual cakes. I taught them a couple of fun techniques, and before long we had some colorful masterpieces on our hands.

Finally, when the cupcakes were baked and cooled, I passed off several bags of bright pink frosting and let the girls frost them. I then divided the girls into two teams and they had a race to see which team could arrange their cupcakes in the shape of a flamingo. Things got a little chaotic, but we had our winner in record time.

One thing stood out above all at that amazing party...the girls were a team. They made loads of memories, which all took place in the kitchen. Maybe this idea will work for the kiddos in your life, too. Perhaps it's time for a little birthday party to bring the young ones into your world. They're counting on you to pass the baking torch, after all!

Train up a child
in the way he should go;
even when he is old
he will not depart from it.
PROVERBS 22:6 ESV

Prayer

Father, how precious it is to pour into the lives of our children, grandchildren, and other little ones. I can hardly wait to get started. Give me creative ideas for how I can mentor them, I pray. Amen.

Hot from the Fire

I didn't spend a lot of time in the kitchen as a kid, but what I lacked in cooking and baking skills, I more than made up for in eating skills. This was particularly true when my grandmother would come for a visit. She was petite and quiet and we hardly knew she was in the house at all, until mealtime came around. That woman knew how to cook. More to the point, she knew how to make bread. Hot, tender, melt-in-the-mouth bread. I'd never tasted anything like it, and I've not had anything since that even comes close.

Grandma's recipe was different from most in that the puffy mounds of dough were fried in hot oil instead of baked in the oven. I can remember gathering around the stove with my siblings and mother, listening to the sizzling *pop-pop-pop* as the dough cooked to a golden brown in the hot oil. We would hover close, waiting for the transformation to take place right in front of our eyes.

My grandma had the skill of a trained chef as she watched over her little balls of dough. She knew exactly when and how to flip them and when to pull them from the fire so that they came out perfect every time. I don't recall ever seeing her burn a thing. Oh, how I wish I had her tenacity and skill!

Maybe you feel like those little balls of dough at times. Perhaps you feel as if you've been tossed in the fire and you're about to be consumed. Isn't it comforting to know that God is our Protector? He's hovering over us, just as we children encircled our grandmother, with love and tenderness in His eyes. He's watching closely to make sure everything comes out perfect in the end, with no burnt edges. More than anything, He cares about you. You're His child, after all. And He is making something beautiful out of your situation even now.

> *When you walk through the fire,*
> *you will not be burned;*
> *the flames will not set you ablaze.*
> ISAIAH 43:2 NIV

Lord, I love the special memories I have of my time in the kitchen with my grandmother. I wouldn't trade them for anything. I also love the image of You hovering close. You're my Guardian, my Protector, my Provision. I would never make it without You, Father. I'm so grateful for Your care. Amen.

Pie Crust Cookies

In Mama's house, nothing went to waste. She knew just how many ingredients to add so that everything worked out right. She had a family of five to feed, after all. The only time I saw her deliberately over-shoot with her ingredients was on pie-baking day. But she had a strategy even then.

Mama used the leftover bits of pie crust to create magical little cinnamon-sugar roll-up cookies. I loved to watch her as she reached for that rolling pin and leveled out the dough. I couldn't take my eyes off her as she sprinkled it with cinnamon and sugar and rolled it up into a long cylinder shape.

The best part? Watching her slice those tiny pinwheel cookies. They were pure perfection, as was everything Mama made. She placed them on a cookie sheet and baked them until they were just perfect—gorgeous, crisp bites of heaven.

My first few nibbles of a warm pinwheel were always pure delight. It melted in the mouth, its crisp edges burning my tongue because I couldn't wait until they had cooled down adequately before having one. The combination of cinnamon and sugar added the perfect touch. I loved them as a child, and now, as I approach my golden years, I love them just as much. I can't eat one without thinking of my mother, without remembering how frugal she was, how careful with every last ingredient.

In many ways, God's workings in my life remind me of how my mother lived. The Lord doesn't let anything go to waste. He takes what I give Him and multiplies it many times over. His "taste and see" approach feels very familiar to me, and I'm grateful for it.

Maybe you've been waiting on the back burner for years, wondering if you'll ever be used. Perhaps you're feeling overlooked, as if you're nothing more than unusable scraps. God won't let your time, talents, or treasures go to waste. Even now He's got a plan to make something beautiful out of every area of your life.

We are his workmanship,
created in Christ Jesus for good works,
which God prepared beforehand,
that we should walk in them.
EPHESIANS 2:10 ESV

Prayer

Father, thank You for multiplying my gifts and abilities. I'm grateful that You find value in me. I want to be used by You, Lord, that others might come to know You. Amen.

Berry-Picking and Cobbler-Baking

Things were different in the olden days when I was a kid. Parents kept us on a much longer leash. We were allowed to roam the neighborhood, play with neighbors several streets away, even ride our bikes in the street. Because I lived in a wooded area, I was allowed to do something else, too...pick berries.

I always got so excited when berry-picking season came around. (I even love it to this day.) As kids, my siblings, friends, and I would pack a lunch, grab our Easter buckets, and head out into the woods for hours on end. I remember crossing muddy ditches, wading through swamps, and having encounters with snakes, all so that we could fill our buckets with those luscious dewberries. By the time we got home in the late afternoon, our fingers were purple from the juice and our bellies were full from all the berries we'd popped in our mouths (completely unwashed, of course).

My mother was always thrilled when we walked through the door with buckets and buckets of berries. After giving them a thorough wash, she would bag them up and put them into the freezer for later use. We ate them over ice cream, we ate them with milk and sugar, but mostly we ate them in Mama's homemade cobblers.

Even now I love a good cobbler, but nothing comes close to the ones Mama made. How she could take a simple crust and berries and turn them into such a spectacular dessert, I'll never know. She managed to get just the right sweetness, something I wasn't able to conquer when I grew up. Mine always turned out too tart, even after the addition of a lot of sugar. Trust me, I kept adding more and more.

Maybe you can relate to that cobbler conundrum, in a relationship with someone who's a little sour, much like those berries. Perhaps this is even someone in your own family or inner circle. You keep adding sugar on top of sugar, hoping to sweeten the relationship, but it takes time and patience to get there. Don't give up! Hopefully your persistence will pay off and lead to a sweet outcome.

> *To the contrary,*
> *"if your enemy is hungry, feed him;*
> *if he is thirsty, give him something to drink;*
> *for by so doing you will heap burning coals*
> *on his head."*
> ROMANS 12:20 ESV

Prayer

People are worth it, Lord...even the tough ones. I'll go on adding sugar to those tough relationships until things improve. I won't give up unless You tell me to. I want to be a friend, even to those who make it difficult. May I follow Your lead. Amen.

Christmas Candy

I have so many wonderful memories of hours spent in my grandmother's kitchen. She really knew how to make kids feel welcome. By far my favorite time of the year at her house was Christmastime. She and my mother passed down a generations-old family tradition that still warms my heart when I remember it. Every year like clockwork, they made Christmas candy.

Most people make sweet Christmas treats like peppermint bark or peanut butter balls, divinity or fudge. Not my grandmother. She had an amazing recipe for hard candy that she never deviated from. The process would start with boiling sugar and water on the stove. I don't remember all the particulars, but at some point, when the concoction reached just the right stage, she would add a few drops of food coloring and heavy-duty extract. The addition of those ingredients caused little bubbles to dance on the surface of the mixture. We had so much fun coming up with the various colors to match the flavors. The cinnamon batch was colored red, peppermint was usually blue, spearmint was green, and so on.

What happened next was both dangerous and mesmerizing. Mama prepped cookie sheets with powdered sugar, and the boiling liquid was poured onto the sheet. The second it was cool enough to handle, we started cutting the now-thickening candy into slivers about the size of a tootsie-roll. I can't tell you how many times I got my little fingers burned, but it was worth every blister. Those jars of powdered sugar–covered hard candies were a staple. We gave them as gifts to teachers, neighbors, pastors, and church friends. What we didn't keep for ourselves, anyway.

I've thought about my blistered fingers many times since then. Some tasks are hard. They require a lot of us. But in the end, it's worth it. Some relationships are tough. They leave us feeling blistered at times. But if we persevere, we will come out on the other end with memories that will last a lifetime.

> *How sweet are your words to my taste,*
> *sweeter than honey to my mouth!*
> PSALM 119:103 ESV

Prayer

Lord, I learned so much from my grandmother. She worked swiftly, so that her hands didn't get burned. May I follow her lead, tackling even the most difficult (and painful) tasks with swift and ready fingers. I know the outcome will be sweet if I don't give up. I praise You for helping me persevere. Amen.

Train Up a Grandchild in the Way He Should Go

I'm a great believer in passing on gifts to the next generation—or even the generation after that. And with nine grandchildren, I've got a lot of gift-passing to do!

My granddaughters especially love to spend time with me in the kitchen. They're almost as passionate about mixing, baking, and decorating as I am. I've planned elaborate baking parties with them, but there have also been a lot of impromptu baking dates as well.

Perhaps the hardest moments are when I'm baking for a customer and the grandkids want to "help." I have to be very careful not to let sticky little fingers find their way into the mixing bowl. And there's always the risk of a kiddo stealing the merchandise and eating it.

Still, there's much to be said for training as you go. On those days when I can spend a few casual hours in the kitchen with the grandkids, we always have such an amazing time. I can almost sense the excitement in their little voices as they offer to help. It warms my heart to know that they love being with me, creating sweet treats together. Sure, they love the cakes and cookies, but at the end of the day one thing is very clear to me—they just love hanging out with me.

Maybe that's how God feels. On those days when I spend intimate time with Him, His heart must feel a lot like mine does when the grandkids are over. When I let Him know—through the joy in my voice, the excitement of my praise—that I am tickled to be with Him, His heart must soar.

Do you love to spend time hanging out with God? Is your relationship so comfortable, so sweet, that hours go by and you don't even realize it? That's how it is when you're in relationships with others, when you love them with your whole heart. You just can't get enough of each other.

When you pray, go into your room and shut the door
and pray to your Father who is in secret.
And your Father who sees
in secret will reward you.
MATTHEW 6:6 ESV

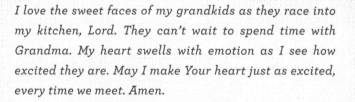

I love the sweet faces of my grandkids as they race into my kitchen, Lord. They can't wait to spend time with Grandma. My heart swells with emotion as I see how excited they are. May I make Your heart just as excited, every time we meet. Amen.

Nuts about Nuts

Before a pecan pie can become a pecan pie, someone has to gather and shell those nuts. Before a caramel-pecan turtle can ever see the light of day, someone has to make a commitment to make sure the pecans are prepped and ready.

That's where my kids come in.

Years ago, my mother lived in the country. Her vast backyard boasted what to us seemed like the world's largest pecan tree. It was heavy with pecans. In fact, the pecans fell at such a crazy rate that you were liable to get whacked on the head if you walked underneath the tree. My children loved to gather the pecans for us. They didn't realize it was work. They simply loved to see who could collect the most in their little plastic bags. We made a game of it and hundreds of pecans were picked up in record time. They looked like squirrels, hoarding for the winter.

Carrying their stash inside the house always made them feel like a million bucks...until they realized that all those nuts had to be shelled. At this point, they bowed out of the game and the adults stepped in.

This nut-gathering game reminds me a lot of what happens when we spread the gospel. Did you know that it takes an average of seven attempts before a person finally comes to a relationship with the Lord? Some people are seed planters (like the one who planted that big pecan tree). Others are waterers. They keep the message alive. Still others (like my children) are gatherers. They're there for the harvest. Some are there for the hard work of discipling. And many are called to bear fruit, like the pecan breaking forth from its shell. They happen along at just the right time to lead someone to the Lord.

What do you consider yourself? Are you a planter? A waterer? A discipler? Are you bold enough to pray for people and lead them to the Lord? Bringing in the harvest is a great honor. Aren't you glad you get to play a role?

> *And he said to them,*
> *"The harvest is plentiful,*
> *but the laborers are few.*
> *Therefore pray earnestly*
> *to the Lord of the harvest*
> *to send out laborers*
> *into his harvest."*
> LUKE 10:2 ESV

Prayer

Father, what a blessing, to be used by You to reach others for the kingdom. I'm not sure where I fall on the spectrum, whether I'm a planter or a reaper, but I'm happy to be of service. Thank You for making me usable, Lord. Amen.

A Shared Kitchen

I love a shared kitchen. Whether I've opened my home to a houseful of grandchildren, a passel of baking-themed partygoers, a friend who happens by, or a loved one who wants to borrow my baking pans and expertise, it's fun to have someone else to chat with while I'm working. The hours go by much quicker when there's laughter in the room.

Many times I've laughed with a baking companion until we've cried. Equally as many times, I've shared life's challenges and woes as we worked together on a baking assignment or tidied up my kitchen after a cookie spree.

When you bring someone else into your home kitchen, you're saying, "I'm comfortable with you. I don't care if you see a few messy dishes or notice that my oven needs to be cleaned. It doesn't matter if my kitchen floor is sticky from powdered sugar or if I have frosting on my blouse. I'm just happy to have you here."

When you open your home in this way, you're following the lead of your forefathers (or would that be foremothers?) who visited with neighbors around the kitchen table. Of course, this was before the days of radio, television, Internet, or cell phones, when people truly focused on the ones they were with. They learned together, fellowshipped together, and ate together.

In many ways, you are also following the lead of Jesus, who invited His disciples to join Him around the table for fellowship. He bids us to meet with Him there, as well. There, in that intimate place, facades fade and authentic conversations take place.

Who would you like to invite into your kitchen today? Is there a relationship you want to further develop? Is there an old friend you haven't seen in a while? Do you have a relative in need of companionship? Put together a plan of action to bake something with a loved one and then watch as God opens the door for sweet, quiet conversation, along with some sweet treats.

*Where two or three
are gathered in my name,
there am I among them.*
MATTHEW 18:20 ESV

Prayer

Oh, how I love to spend quiet one-on-one time in the kitchen with my friends, Lord. It's a great place to catch up, to share concerns, and to share deep fellowship. Just as You welcome me to Your table, Lord, I welcome others to mine. Thank You for that wonderful example, Father. Amen.

My Kitchen Mentor

The final week of my mother's life was spent at home under hospice care. She was completely unaware of anything going on around her. She'd drifted into a peaceful sleep, and this uninhibited slumber went on for eight long days while we kept vigil.

The home I shared with Mom filled with people. Family members came from all over the country, converging in that place. We wanted to be together as much as we could.

Others came by, too. Neighbors brought meals. Friends from church showed up with groceries. My pastor's wife even helped me clean the house one morning when my guests were out. The amount of love and compassion poured out on our family was remarkable.

I spent as many hours as I could at my mom's bedside, but during those moments when I stepped outside her room, I still felt the need to play hostess. My usually quiet house was teeming with people, after all. Some slept on mattresses on the floor. Others had suitcases strewn about in the guest room.

Despite the fact that we had plenty of food being brought in, I still felt the need to bake. Each day I prepared something for the crew—a cake, cookies... anything. One particular afternoon I was looking for something different to bake. My sister-in-law told me about one of her favorite recipes, potato chip cookies. I'd never heard of such a thing. She looked up the recipe and led me through the directions. We worked side by side as I learned from her. The cookies were fabulous, unique from any I'd ever had.

It didn't occur to me until later what a gift she'd given me. For years, my mother had mentored me in the kitchen. Now, in the throes of losing her, I'd lost my mentor, my guide. But God stepped in—in the flesh-and-blood form of my sister-in-law—to show me that there was plenty of learning ahead.

Who mentors you? Is there someone you're currently mentoring? Isn't it sweet of the Lord to place us in such wonderful relationships where we continue to learn and grow? May we never get too old or too busy to learn.

> *Your testimonies are my delight;*
> *they are my counselors.*
> PSALM 119:24 ESV

Prayer

Lord, I'm so grateful for the years my mother poured into my life. And I'm grateful for the many—like my sister-in-law—who have stepped up to share their knowledge with me. May I be as generous with others, Father. Amen.

Mama's Cookbook

She used it nearly every time we visited her house in the country. Mama's cookbook was a staple. When its worn cover was pulled back, magical things happened. Sugar cookies came dancing out. Cakes and pies were birthed. Homemade caramel-pecan turtles were formed. Sugary clouds of divinity were created.

All of Mama's secrets were buried in that little book, and it captivated us all. We had so much fun watching her refer to it time and time again.

Since my mother passed away a couple of years back, her cookbook has become one of my most-valued possessions. I keep it close by and turn to it often, particularly when it comes to cookies, cakes, and pies. Knowing how many hours went into those pages, understanding her passion for each dish she shared, brings me such comfort. And seeing those handwritten pages does something to my heart every time. It's as if she's still here with me every time I open that precious book. I see the chocolate pie recipe and I'm reminded of the many times she prepared it for us. My gaze travels to the coconut pecan cake recipe and I remember the time she baked me one for my birthday. Mama's love and care went into that precious book.

In many ways, the Bible reminds me of my mom's cookbook. It has every recipe I need for a good life. God took the time to share every ingredient, every step, everything I could ever need. If I follow the instructions fully, the outcome will be sweet. I simply need to stick to the recipes He's already given me.

When I read the Word, I see His handprint all over it. I'm reminded of the many times He's made Himself real to me. It's a very real and present reminder that He is still right here with me. And He's here with You, too. What a perfect day to turn to His Word for some precious inspiration.

The word of God is living and active,
sharper than any two-edged sword,
piercing to the division of soul and of spirit,
of joints and of marrow,
and discerning the thoughts
and intentions of the heart.
HEBREWS 4:12 ESV

Lord, thank You for Your Word! Talk about an amazing collection of life recipes. I'm so glad You passed it down to me, Father. It's a living, breathing legacy, one I'm so thrilled to possess. Amen.

Snickerdoodles

This is my mom's recipe, and I love it! At first I balked at the idea of using shortening (instead of butter), but I quickly learned that shortening gives the cookie its light, fluffy texture.

MIX TOGETHER

- 1 cup shortening
- 2 eggs
- 1 cup sugar

IN A SEPARATE BOWL, SIFT

- 2¾ cups flour
- 2 teaspoons cream of tartar
- 1 teaspoon baking soda
- ½ teaspoon salt

INSTRUCTIONS

Combine ingredients.

Shape dough into 1-inch balls. Roll in cinnamon-and-sugar mixture (2 tablespoons sugar and 2 tablespoons cinnamon).

Place 2 inches apart on ungreased cookie sheet. Bake for 10 minutes at 375°F.

Mom's Coconut-Meringue Pie

INGREDIENTS

- 1 cup sugar
- ¼ cup cornstarch
- ¼ teaspoon salt
- 3 cups milk
- 3 eggs, separated
- 2 tablespoons butter
- 1½ teaspoons vanilla
- 1½ cups coconut

INSTRUCTIONS

Combine sugar, cornstarch, and salt. Gradually stir in milk. Cook in microwave in 5-minute increments until the mixture thickens, stirring as needed. Beat egg yolks separately. Add 1 cup hot mixture to egg yolks and stir, then add the remainder of the hot mixture. Cook in microwave 2 more minutes. Stir in butter, vanilla, and coconut. Pour into baked pie shell. Top with meringue. (See recipe for meringue on the following page.)

Mom's Meringue Recipe

INGREDIENTS

- 4 egg whites
- 1 cup hot water
- 6 tablespoons sugar
- 1 tablespoon cornstarch

INSTRUCTIONS

Whip egg whites until they form a soft peak. Set aside. Cook water, sugar, and cornstarch until thick. Add quickly to egg whites while beating for 30 seconds. Spoon on pie. Bake at 350°F until golden.

Miss Elba's Potato Chip Cookies

INGREDIENTS

- 1 lb butter
- 1½ cups sugar
- 1 teaspoon vanilla
- 3 cups flour
- Pinch of salt
- 1½ cups crushed Ruffles potato chips (thickly crushed by hand)
- 1 cup chopped pecans
- Powdered sugar

INSTRUCTIONS

Cream together butter, sugar, and vanilla. Slowly mix in the flour and salt. Stir in Ruffles and pecans. Drop by spoonfuls onto parchment-lined cookie sheet. Flatten dough with a wet fork. Bake at 325°F for 12–15 minutes. Sprinkle with powdered sugar while hot. Cool on wire rack.

Double Chocolate Mint Chocolate Chip Cookies

CREAM TOGETHER

- ½ cup salted butter
- ½ cup shortening
- ¾ cup sugar
- ¾ cup packed brown sugar
- 2 eggs

SIFT TOGETHER IN SEPARATE BOWL

- 2½ cups flour
- ¾ cup cocoa powder
- 1 teaspoon baking soda

MERGE INGREDIENTS.

ADD

- 1 bag Andes mint chocolate chips
- ½ cup chocolate chips

Scoop by spoonful onto parchment-lined cookie sheets.

Bake at 375°F for 12 minutes (approximately), turning the tray at the midway point to assure perfect coloring.

TOP TEN TIPS
FOR TRAINING LITTLE BAKERS

1. Let the kids know they are welcome in your space, that it's their space too.

2. Safety first! Keep little fingers away from mixer blades, hot ovens, and stovetops.

3. Have tasks laid out in advance so the kids have a "real" job to do while baking with you.

4. Teach as you go. Explain in kid-friendly terms what you're doing and why you're doing it. Be ready to stop at any given point to share details.

5. Don't be afraid to let the kids help. Instead of keeping them on the fringes, let them add the ingredients to the mixer or scoop the cookies onto the tray. Who cares if things aren't perfect in the end? They're on a learning curve and truly want to grow and develop their skills.

6. Teach children to follow a recipe so that they will be able to bake on their own sooner rather than later.

7. Teach the kiddos how to measure and convert. (Double a recipe and have them help you figure out the amounts you'll need.)

8. Don't let the baking day turn into a free-for-all. Maintain control and give boundaries.

9. Encourage all artistic endeavors, but also give gentle correction/instruction when necessary.

10. Share family recipes that have come down from parents and grandparents.

Clever Baking Hacks

- Need to add butter to your flour mixture but can't work it in without creating a mess? Grate the cold butter first and then add it to your dry ingredients.

- For a better outcome, use eggs that are several days old.

- Need to get a piece of eggshell out of your batter? Use another larger piece of eggshell to fetch it.

- Peel fresh ginger by scraping a spoon against the skin. It should come right off.

- Soften butter quickly by placing in the microwave for 10–15 seconds per stick.

- Dip your cookie cutters in flour before each use to avoid stickiness.

- Make your own powdered sugar by combining 1 cup granulated sugar and 1 tablespoon cornstarch in a food processor.

- Looking for a moister cake? Add a tablespoon or two of mayonnaise to your batter. It won't affect the taste and will give that cake the moisture you're craving.

- Hungry for cookies but don't have any flour on hand? Reach for a cake mix. Add ½ cup oil and 2 eggs and you'll have the perfect consistency for cookie dough.

DaySpring

LIVE YOUR FAITH

Dear Friend,

This book was prayerfully crafted with you, the reader, in mind—every word, every sentence, every page—was thoughtfully written, designed, and packaged to encourage you...right where you are this very moment. At DaySpring, our vision is to see every person experience the life-changing message of God's love. So, as we worked through rough drafts, design changes, edits and details, we prayed for you to deeply experience His unfailing love, indescribable peace, and pure joy. It is our sincere hope that through these Truth-filled pages your heart will be blessed, knowing that God cares about you—your desires and disappointments, your challenges and dreams.

He knows. He cares. He loves you unconditionally.

BLESSINGS!
THE DAYSPRING BOOK TEAM